ENTREPRENEUR ROCKET FUEL:

How Startup Founders Recruit World-class Talent and Build Culture to Transform Their Business

Entrepreneur Rocket Fuel: How Startup Founders Recruit World-class Talent and Build Culture to Transform Their Business

© Copyright 2018 by Rob Kornburn

FREE BONUS

Hiring and retaining an A team is so important to the success of your startup. Because everyone learns and applies knowledge a little differently, we created a website with bonus content.

This content will help you on your journey to creating an amazing startup team, and an amazing startup company.

The bonuses are 100% free for readers of this book.

You get access at
www.entrepreneurrocketfuel.com/bonus

This is what you will receive:

- Culture & Values worksheet
- Top hiring and culture tips from Founders & CEOs
- Personal Operating Manual for new employees
- Hiring Pipeline Worksheet for CEOs and Founders
- Examples of good "Careers" pages
- Examples of Good Job Descriptions
- And more

You can get everything at
www.entrepreneurrocketfuel.com/bonus

Thank you so much for taking the time to check it out.

Table of Contents

Why Write This Book

A huge percentage of new businesses fail.

The exact statistics are hard to find, but estimates range as high as an 80% or 90% failure rate within the first five years. I am a true believer in entrepreneurship and its ability to positively impact people's lives and improve economies. So I hate that high failure rate, it drives me crazy. All these entrepreneurs, trying to change the world, and unable to make it.

There has been a ton of good advice, writing, education and a general movement based around improving and testing your product idea. This is called the "Lean Startup" movement; many of these methods are taught in most of the best business schools in the world such as MIT, Stanford, and Kellogg. (If you are not familiar with this term, buy and read Eric Reis' book *The Lean Startup*).

But beyond improving and testing your idea, there is one HUGE thing you can do to improve your odds of creating a successful business, and that is to get the *best team possible* working in your company. Unlike your idea, or the market, or capital providers, or competition, your team is almost 100% within your control.

If you improve your team, you improve your odds of creating a great company and changing the world. It is that simple.

I used to be a venture capitalist ("VC") and a founder. These days, I advise startup companies, both informally through accelerator programs and business schools, and formally as a paid executive coach to high-growth founders.

The **Number One Challenge** that I hear from CEOs is how hard it is to hire great people. So it's the most difficult thing that founders have to do, and it dramatically increases the odd of success.

The funny thing is, I am not trained as an HR professional or an organizational psychologist, other than being part of great teams and building my own. In fact, when I was in business school, I HATED my Organizational Behavior classes. I just didn't get it. Org charts and structures sounded like so much blah blah blah.

After becoming a VC, I saw firsthand the importance of the team in the success of every startup company.

After I left the venture capital profession, I became an operating executive and an entrepreneur. THAT is where I really saw team, teamwork, and culture in action. I saw the good—great teams pulling together to create products, to sell, to win, and to support customers. I also saw the bad—poor teams (team members) or misaligned incentives which kept some companies from really achieving greatness.

In addition to my own personal experiences, I also was lucky enough to work for many years in the *business* of hiring, as an executive in human capital and recruitment companies like Monster.com and Bullhorn, one of the leading software platforms for professional recruiters. I have also been an advisor and board member to a number of innovative HR technology and hiring companies.

As I started to do some thinking about best practices, I looked for a great book about hiring and culture in startups and could not find one. I found some books about hiring in general. But hiring in larger companies is not even close to the same as hiring in startups.

Startups have almost no budget to spend on recruiters and don't have HR teams. Startups need to hire rapidly to meet technology and market windows, and startups need to get it right. The wrong team can sink your company.

The great books about being a startup CEO touched on hiring, but not with the depth that I think the subject needs. After all, it one of the biggest challenges, and it has a HUGE impact on success.

This book isn't perfect. I interviewed a lot of people who I thought were either experts, or were great team builders, or who had fantastic approaches to building culture.

I called on many of my friends and network to create this book, people who know more about creating and scaling great teams than I do. I also included interviews from CEOs I know or have met.

There are a bunch of cool bonuses related to the book that you can find at www.entrepreneurrocketfuel.com/bonus. You can also subscribe to my blog posts to learn more and stay up to speed on my latest thinking about team-building, scaling, strategy, and fund raising, which are the areas I focus on in my private coaching.

In addition to those bonuses, you can find lots of other insights on startups at my blog:

www.startlaunchgrow.com

I also encourage you to join my private Facebook group if you want to be part of a supportive, thriving community of high-growth entrepreneurs:

Facebook Group: Startup Growth Community

I work personally with a very small number of clients as a coach, on team-building, fundraising, and executive leadership. You can learn more about that here.

Why Team Is So Important

As a startup founder, you are faced with a nearly impossible set of tasks. You are trying to build an innovative product, find and satisfy customers, bring in capital, and build a world-class team.

You need to build a team who will bring your product ideas to market, while battling on three fronts: limited money, limited time, and no brand. Specifically, in terms of your team:

- You need to add people who can shoulder some of the workload and who provide expertise that you do not have.

- Your team's past experience and credentials need to help convince investors so you can raise outside capital.

- You need to build a culture and workplace environment that is fun, challenging, resilient, and enjoyable in order to attract and retain "A-level" talent.

In my work as an investor, a startup founder, and now as a coach to founders and teams, I have found that a great team isn't just the group of people who will build the company. They are literally the third leg of the stool, probably the most important, of startup success.

"No way!" you say. "The product is the most important thing, not the team. A company with a bad product and a great team isn't going to succeed, at least not for long." That is true.

But... a company with a great team can build, or rebuild and rebuild, a poor product. That same great team can find a new market, or a new business model if the first one isn't working.

Many entrepreneurs believe that product-market fit is their number one challenge. I understand that feeling. After all, without a product that customers want, there *is no business*.

Your target market is your destination. It's where you want to get. It's the far-off planet that you aim to conquer, and your product is the rocket ship. You can't just will yourself there or throw around some "floo powder" like Harry Potter to jet yourself around.

Even if you have an amazing destination, and the most amazing rocket ship in the universe, your rocket will simply sit on the ground without fuel. Or worse, it will not be able to complete the journey.

Your team is **the rocket fuel**. It creates the momentum for the rocket to escape gravity, and for you to course-correct along the way.

In some ways, building an amazing team is *more* important than building a great product. This company is your primary focus and the outcome matters a great deal to you, but the company is only one piece of your career.

You will move on to other parts of your career, either by creating more companies, doing philanthropy, becoming an angel investor, or doing something totally different outside the startup world. Regardless of your path, you will almost certainly call on your network to help propel your new activity. You might even call on them more than once.

A great network is invaluable. Some say, "Your network is your net worth." Much of your network is going to come from professional contacts, not family or friends, and most of those professional contacts are *people who you have worked with before*.

If you have any doubts, take a look at the powerful Silicon Valley networks. One such group is called "The PayPal Mafia." You would be *incredibly* lucky be part of a group like that. After working at PayPal, the executives went on to found Tesla, Palentir, SpaceX, YouTube, Yelp, Yammer, Reddit, and others, and one is a partner at Sequoia Capital.

The same thing has happened in Boston, New York, Austin, Seattle, and internationally; it isn't just a Silicon Valley phenomenon.

So you may need an amazing Head of Marketing for your current company and that is what you are setting out to hire. But thinking more broadly, you are also hiring someone that you may work with again, or who may be an angel or VC in the future, or she may go on to found her own company. Don't let that thought be daunting—but do let it help inform you about the importance of team for *your whole career.*

I don't pretend to be an HR person. I know it's a hard job. But in being part of great teams, and observing others as a VC and coach, I have come to this conclusion:

> *Hiring an amazing team is a critical skill of the most successful founders. It CANNOT be outsourced to recruiters, and it isn't a human resource function.*

Hiring a great team of amazing people and building a culture that enables them to do amazing work, and gets them to stay at the company, is the job of the CEO and the executive management team. It may be the most challenging part of being a CEO in today's business climate. Almost universally, CEOs will tell you that hiring great people is their number one business problem—beyond more revenue, more technical milestones, and more funding.

Finding a Co-Founder

It's possible that you have already put your founding team in place and are past this phase of company building. If so, congratulations! Go ahead and skip this chapter if you want, especially if you have set up appropriate protections like vesting schedules in case a co-founder leaves the business.

One of the first decisions you'll have to make is whether to start the company yourself or work with co-founders. This decision is deeply personal and impacts the kind of company you build. Starting a flower shop is not the same as building a software startup or biotech company. There are different technical hurdles, different capital requirements, different marketing and sales features, and exit paths.

Second, your decision to work with co-founders or fly solo will be impacted not only by the type of business, but by who you are and what you love to do. Some entrepreneurs will go it alone until they have some traction, then seek co-founders.

Third, if you can add to the overall skills of the team, that is a great reason to add a co-founder. Compatibility is important, but not sufficient. Don't just partner with or hire people because they are friends. To succeed, you will likely need to add critical skills in marketing, product development, finance, sales, and design.

Co-founders are great sounding boards for handling challenging decisions. Rather than having to work through problems on your own, a co-founder can help you think things through. They can help you see alternate approaches and run scenarios.

Angel investor Reid Hoffman, co-founder of LinkedIn, suggests that media have built up startup founders as supermen and superwomen. He spoke of this concern in a lecture at Stanford University in 2014:

> "One way, I think, to explode the myth of super-founder is [that] usually it's best to have two or three people on a team rather than a solo founder. It's not to say that solo founders don't actually play out and they can, successfully, but most often two or three people is much better.
>
> When I look at these things as an investor, and..[ask], "What is a good composition of a project and founders that are likely to succeed[?]", it's usually two or three of them....what great founders do is seek the networks that will be essential to their task..."

Co-founders contribute to the culture of the business and help you reinforce those values when you hire staff. It is much easier to share accountability than to have it all on your own shoulders. A co-founder is there with you when things go off track. It's like training for a marathon together, or having a support team when you're trying to lose a few pounds. Someone is in it with you, and that provides emotional lift.

When I began my first startup I didn't really think this through or deeply enough. Going it alone turned out to be far more difficult and lonelier than I expected.

If you decide to work with a co-founder, these are some initial questions to ask yourself:

- In what ways should we be the same, and in what ways should we be different?
- What traits should I look for?
- Have we worked together before?

- Will we work well together? What makes me confident of that?

- Can we give it a trial run?

- How do they react when things don't work out?

- What would excite them in terms of an exit?

- Would I want to be stuck in an airport with this person (the 'Airport test')?

You don't have to like each other, but you do have to respect each other and make decisions collaboratively. There will be make-it-or-break-it decisions that will come up. Sometimes you'll disagree. If you're not sure, the important thing is to keep an open mind and start moving the company forward. It might become clearer as you progress and start to hit obstacles.

Mark Suster, a two-time founder turned top venture capitalist, thinks it's more important to get started on one's own before trying to find a perfect co-founder.

> "Even if you think you know them, people change...I say, 'go ahead and take the leap' if you want to start a company... Hire your co-founder [later]. Give them a large sum of equity. 20%. 30%. Even 40%. Vested over four years. If you ever fall out of love you have a pre-nuptial agreement... Truly treat them like a co-founder. Give them access to all confidential information. Involve them in fund raising, hiring, strategy, etc. Publicly call them a co-founder."

Finding a co-founder, whether you do it before you start or after, as Suster suggests, is as much an art as a science. You need someone who shares your vision, someone with whom you're compatible, and who wants the same outcome as you. Maybe you don't want a big venture capital-backed company, just a small, sustainable, profitable business.

You and your co-founder should have differences as well. Further on, there are interviews with Sean Byrnes and Edith Harbaugh, two CEOs who went through very different processes to vet their co-founders.

Startup expert and early Apple software evangelist, Guy Kawasaki, suggests that co-founders should differ in expertise, orientation, and perspective.

> "Founders need to complement each other to build a great organization. Some people like to sweat the details (microscopes). Others like to ignore the details and worry about the big issues (telescopes)...The more perspectives, the merrier. These can include young versus old, rich versus poor, male versus female, urban versus country, engineering versus sales, techie versus touchy, Muslim versus Christian, straight versus gay, Android versus iOS, and Macintosh versus Windows."

If you are trying to find and vet a co-founder, the most important thing is to have some kind of process, a set of things that you are trying to uncover and a way to uncover them. You clearly want to understand their capabilities but also their values.

Make sure that you are aligned around your incentives for starting the business and what you want out of it, how you prefer to work and communicate, what roles and equity you will have, what values and culture you want to develop, and more.

This isn't something to just gloss over. Noam Wasserman of Harvard Business School studied the subject extensively for his book, *The Founder's Dilemmas*. Wasserman found that 65 percent of high-potential startup companies failed as a result of conflict among the co-founders.

To see a set of questions to help you work through these issues with potential co-founders, you can check them out at www.entrepreneurrocketfuel.com/bonus.

What VCs Think About Your Team

"Bet on the jockey, not the horse."

Translation: Invest in the team rather than the idea

Venture capitalists assess prospective startup investments on a number of areas: your **product**, your **market**, and your **team**. Many VCs view your **team** as the most important of the these.

Jeff Crowe, General Partner at Norwest Venture Partners, said that he thought the team was the most important element they considered in making a new investment in an early-stage company. (See Jeff's interview next.)

Amit Raizada from Vision Venture Partners wrote, "Like most VCs, I'll invest in a B idea with an A team, rather than an A idea with a B team."[1]

Rebecca Kaden, General Partner at Union Square Ventures, was asked in an interview with 33Voices about a CEO's top three priorities and what they should be. According to Kaden, they are:

1. Hiring and Retaining the Team

2. Customer obsession throughout the organization

3. Make sure you don't run out of money

Kaden added that she evaluates not only the team "as is," but also closely evaluates their ability to hire:

---

[1] Fast Company.com, 07/20/2017, https://www.fastcompany.com/40442339/this-vc-explains-how-to-avoid-pitching-good-ideas-badly

"Hiring even part of your absolute dream management team will optimize your chance for success more than anything else."

Why do VCs care so much about the team?

The team is absolutely crucial for VCs because products and markets can change, but great teams are capable of adapting to those changes. It is quite common for a great team to find a different market from the one they first envision, to change their business model, or try a new product approach in the same market.

Most of us are familiar with the concept of "pivoting" or moving to a new business after the first concept did not succeed. When you see a truly successful pivot, the constant in all of those is the team.

Groupon, Pinterest, Flickr, PayPal, Slack, and Twitter are all examples of a great team pivoting to success after their initial idea didn't produce customer success.

Twitter, for example, started as a podcast subscription network called Odeo. Podcasting was taking off based on the huge success of Apple's iPod and iTunes store. After Apple announced that it would include a podcasting platform built into every iPod, the Odeo founders Jack Dorsey, Biz Stone, and Evan Williams built an SMS group text system called Twittr. The initial traction was propelled forward by a lucky random event: the fact that Twttr users spread the word about a small earthquake that had hit San Francisco. (Eventually, the name changed.)

Even in situations lacking a pivot from the original idea, the team is the crucial element that takes the company from idea to business, from interesting product concept to a company that delights and serves its customers.

"Ideas are cheap, execution is everything." - Chris Sacca, former Shark on the hit show *Shark Tank,*

and angel investor in Uber, Twitter, Instagram, and Kickstarter

Only with a great team will you get great execution. Great teams can:

- Launch amazing products that fit the customer's pain
- Produce great marketing campaigns
- Sell effectively
- Manage cash appropriately
- Recruit to grow
- Produce amazing customer service

So, if "the team" is a crucial element to VC decision-making, what exactly are they looking for?

It all starts with the CEO. The CEO is THE leader and the primary person backed by the VC fund. Although VCs sometimes get a reputation for firing founding CEOs, the truth is that many VCs won't even consider funding a company unless they think the CEO will be the leader for the foreseeable future. They want the CEO to grow and succeed as the business grows. When the investment is made, the fund is backing the CEO and likely believes that you can take the company through to an exit. Replacing a CEO is done as a last resort, typically because the company isn't growing effectively or because the Board and investors has lost confidence in the CEO.

VCs look for a team that has complementary skills and that they believe can work well together. Let's take each of these points separately.

Skills

Venture capitalists look for a certain set of skills in a CEO, and a different skillset in the team that they are backing.

For CEOs, VCs want to see market vision, strategic intelligence, drive, will to win, salesmanship, magnetism/attraction, common sense, and coachability.

It may not be possible to find CEOs with all of these skills or traits. As a VC, I would not compromise on market vision and salesmanship. Even with a great technical team and product lead, a CEO without market vision will not be able to set an effective strategy for the company. Market vision also enables the team to determine the best business model for the company. Other than product market fit, the go-to-market model (business model) is probably the most important decision that a startup will make.

Salesmanship and magnetism are different versions of the same skill. Being an effective salesperson may be the largest part of a CEO's job, because CEOs are constantly selling. They sell early (and large) customers as much or more than salespeople. They convince investors that the company can be a big success and the investor will make a lot of money. They sell strategic partners who can bring complementary technology or channels. And they sell prospective employees to come and join on the crazy ride.

In addition to the CEO's skills, the VCs will also want to see someone who is capable of effectively *delivering* the product to customers. In a software, internet, Web, mobile or e-commerce company, that person is usually CTO or VP of Engineering. In a biotech or hard-science type company, that person is a research head, chief scientist, or principal investigator. This role is crucial because this person is responsible for making sure critical technical milestones are met.

The other crucial role in a product-oriented company is marketing, though at this point, you might not need a CMO or high-powered executive. You will want a mid-level *scrappy* marketer who personally manages many different ways of getting your company known to customers, and generates leads for the business over and above the founders' personal networks.

The rest of the founding and early team will vary significantly; titles and hierarchy are not really relevant at this point. What matters most is that the team is aligned against the biggest risks of the business. Sean Byrnes, founder of Outlier.ai (interviewed later in this book), said that he tried to focus different team members on "company-killing risks."

Working Relationship

It is often said that taking venture capital is more like a marriage than a business partnership. When you bring investors into your company, you are going to be partners with those investors for the next 8 to10 years., Your VC is likely to be on your Board of Directors, so they (and the other board members) can fire you and set your compensation.

But the nature of the partnership goes so much deeper than that. The VC can offer help in a number of ways:

- Help you raise your next round of funding
- Help you recruit team members
- Give you strategic advice
- Coach you to improve your own execution and performance as an executive
- Pick you up in tough times (through the vast highs and lows)
- Provide a sounding board when there are gut-wrenching decisions to make

Experienced VC partners are looking for a CEO with whom they can build a good working relationship. You don't need to like the partner socially, and the partner doesn't need to like you, but you need to understand each other's frame of reference with the ability to work through issues and differences of opinion together. You need a respectful relationship with strong EQ on both sides.

In my time as a VC, I had strong relationships with my portfolio CEOs and would never have backed the company if I did not. In one situation, we agreed up front that the founding CEO would move to a different role and we would *jointly* find a new leader for the business.

As a founding CEO, I tried very hard to only work with VCs with whom I thought I could build a great relationship, probably because (luckily) I had seen how powerful that could be. It was an incredibly powerful vote of confidence for the VC partner to say that they intended to back me again, whether this particular company worked or not. It made me want to produce even more for the fund (and myself, of course).

In summary, investors are assessing whether your team has unique insight into the customer and their pain, the ability to produce a world-class solution around that pain, the resilience to withstand multiple challenges, and the ability to continue to scale and hire more and more A players as you grow. Addressing these questions well will put you on the path to raising outside capital.

Interview with Jeff Crowe, General Partner, Norwest Venture Partners

Jeff Crowe is the Managing Partner of Norwest Venture Partners. Jeff has been a venture capitalist since 2004 and has been on the "Midas List" of top VCs five times. Prior to joining Norwest, Jeff was President & COO of Dovebid, and Founder and CEO of Edify Inc.

Rob Kornblum
So maybe start at the beginning when you're looking at a new deal. Tell me about how you think about team versus idea versus market.

Jeff Crowe:
Sure. So that's exactly kind of the triangle that we consider. Sometimes we lump idea and market together, but it is very much team, idea, market. And for us to make an investment in the company, especially [at the] early stage, we have to feel very good about all three. We especially have to feel good about the team. Not all venture firms necessarily feel that way. Sometimes they feel like, "Gee, if the team's going after a good enough market and the market's important enough, then a big enough, good enough market will drag along any team." Maybe that was true 10 or 20 years ago, but now I find that there's so much capital and so many teams going after any market or any ideas, that you really have to have a good team even if you have a good market because you're going to attract a lot of competition very, very quickly.

Also, if there's a slight pivot, or maybe a major pivot involved, that really depends upon the team's ability to recognize the need to change course.

So it's really all about execution.

It's all execution. And often times success is driven by [the] product market fit, which is driven by the original vision of the team. And so it keeps coming back to the team, whether it's vision, product market fit, or execution. I don't make an investment unless I think that the CEO of the team I'm investing in is the CEO who can take the business for a long way.

I don't subscribe to, "Let's swap out the CEO a year from now." At least in the businesses where I invest, that's usually akin to brain surgery. I don't want to make an investment thinking I'll have to execute brain surgery along the way. It's just too hard.

When you assess a team, what are the elements you look for? What makes a great team?

Well, I start with the CEO. Sometimes the founding CEO has amazing co-founders; sometimes the co-founders are okay, and that becomes a discussion, but if the CEO's amazing enough, then we've ridden with that sometimes with great success.

But when it comes to CEOs, they have to be action-oriented, driven by a compelling product market vision; they have to live, eat, and breathe that vision. They have to have very strong business judgment and be very practically minded, and get a lot done with modest amounts of capital.

They have to be able to sell their vision and attract other top-notch employees. They have to be able to sell customers, whatever that means, and investors, and business partners, so they have to be very compelling in the articulation of their vision in their product.

So we've run into founders who are very good at some of these, but not good at others; some CEOs can't get stuff done, or are too theoretical (not really practical in their business judgment or their business thinking), or can't quite articulate the vision quite well enough to attract top-notch people. And we've learned over the years that the best founders, the CEOs, really have to have this whole package. And if you're missing key pieces of it, isn't going to work.

So you try to go through a process of discovery by spending enough time with the CEO to really understand all these characteristics and do enough reference checking. And when you have to make a decision sometimes in two weeks, it can be tough to make that decision accurately as a Venture Investor or make it with enough information, but that's the type of projection you're trying to make.

If the CEO has the product vision, then there's usually a technology co-founder. We get quite nervous if there's no technology co-founder, because we wonder why the business and product co-founder can't attract a high-quality technology co-founder. And if you get a substandard technology co-founder that means you're going to go through some kind of painful rewrite or re-architecture downstream.

And any other things you look for in the early stages?

[I look at the team's] compatibility. Sometimes there are three or four [co-founders]. There can be an ops person or couple [of] product people involved. We really look also at their compatibility, their ability to kind of work together...and divide and conquer because you have to move so fast. We're trying to understand their "marriage," if you will. [They will] spend so much time together; sometimes teams just kind of combust within a year or two, [which] can be very painful.

Too much heat.

Right. You're also trying to understand what kind of culture that team is going to build. Cultures are usually the extensions of the personalities, and the values, and the visions of the founding team. Are they super high integrity, do they really care about people, do they want have ethics and transparency in everything they do? At the same time, are they feeling inclusive, are they building a strong community, can they communicate and collocate those values across everybody? Can they hire people who share those values, but have yet very diverse points of view? It's a whole series of things.

We've seen companies which seem to check a lot of the boxes, then blow up because of cultures that became systemic extensions of dysfunction in the personalities of the founders. And after two or three years, those ended up being recipes for disaster; it manifested itself and they sell out. We try to pay a lot of attention to that as well.

In the most successful teams, you mentioned the ability to sell and attract. What are some of the common things that you've seen, as companies have been successful and scaled, that other teams can try to replicate?

Sure. CEOs have to be very, very clear thinking [and] clear-eyed about the right team members at the right points in the company's growth and evolution. And often times the people who are well suited to be with you very early on may not be the same set of people who are well suited at the company's mid-point [size], or when the company's much, much larger. Team members can self-select out, but often they don't. Often there's tremendous loyalty from the CEO to the team members, based on their major contributions, but sometimes the CEOs have to make very tough decisions.

So just to give you a current example, just happened in one of my software companies, where the original VP of sales was brought in shortly after the founding; he did a great job taking the company to $20 million of annual revenue, the CEO judged that this individual would not [be able to get the company] from $20 [million] to $100 [million]. Just very different skill sets around process, around organization, around systems and infrastructure...very, very hard to make a move when you have a VP who's been hitting their numbers throughout to do that.

And yet the CEO convinced the VP of sales to take another role, starting up another region within the company. Just as the CEO was making this move the sales organization started to show cracks. I mean, the timing was brilliant. That is so rare. It's not just from a perspective as a Venture Investor, but having been a CEO for nine years, your loyalty to people who have achieved for you [and worked hard for you] often supersedes your judgment about, "Are they going to be the right person for the next phase of the company?"

One of my successful companies, LendingClub, basically had three evolutions of the management team in the run-up to going public.

And through that, the CEO did a very nice job of [transitioning]: early, mid, and late. Had he not made those transitions, the company would not have successfully scaled to the point of going public. And well-functioning, experienced boards, who have enough knowledge of the situation and good relationships with the CEO, can help the CEO understand that. Sometimes it requires people who are not so personally close to each individual to sit down and discuss with the CEO, "Who on this team can [and can't] scale for going from $20 to $100 million in the next three years? Let's step back and go through that discussion." And really experienced, talented CEOs will do that themselves, but many CEOs get so busy with the day to day, sometimes the boards can help.

The most successful CEOs, how much time do they spend on recruiting or on people matters? A third of their time, perhaps?

Easily a third of their time. You're managing people as opposed to working directly in product or talking directly to customers. Some CEOs have to make sure they are thoughtful about their time; the people issues can be so much in front of you that you've got to maintain contact with the market, [maintain] contact with technology and product, and not get swamped with just people issues.

As organizations scale, you really have to think about leverage points. As a team, think about bringing in a very high-quality set of lieutenants or direct reports who are going to be managing people beneath you. Where many founding teams can through a painful transition, it's the founders that hire a number of individual contributors who are exceptionally talented. That team just goes and rocks it for a year or two years, and then they start to scale.

All of a sudden, now, you have to start that very critical transition of putting in the next layer of management. The old adage is, "It's very tough to hire people. If you're grade B, it's very tough to hire people grade A beneath you." So as the business scales with grade A founders, bringing grade B next layer directors, that's going to cause a dilution of talent beneath them. So it's exceptionally important to bring in that layer to be as talented as the senior layer. And savvy CEOs can spend an extraordinary amount of time making sure that that next layer comes in as a success, works well together with not only the founders, but up, down, and across the organization.

You see CEOs doing that personally, in terms of interviewing, recruiting people who aren't going to report to them?

Oh, sure. When I was CEO, I interviewed everybody up through the first 100 employees, for A+ talent and a culture fit.

Since cultures and talent can be very different, how do you see your CEOs balancing that combination? It's like you have the rock star who breaks a lot of glass versus the person who's an exceptionally good fit but isn't quite as talented.

Our high-performing companies will often complain about the fact that they have a high bar on both, so it makes it very tough to hire people. Today, I think there is less tolerance than maybe 20 years ago, and more rejections, for people who are exceptional performers but not culture fits. [Often times,] a number of my high-performing companies don't hit their own objectives for pace of hiring, including especially the senior levels because they maintain such a high bar on both fronts. We're getting them to try to hit both.

Are they example of teams that you were confident about, in terms of their composition of founders and their ability to attract?

And I've seen this repeatedly, Rob. Very successful companies, where the CEO [decides to work] with a couple buddies, he's drawing stuff out on napkin, and he says, "Let's go do this." And you divide up the equity and the roles, and then someone like me comes in and says to the CEO, "This idea is great, this market's great. Your co-founders have too much equity and two years from now they're not going to be in these roles." And they get very upset and say, "What do you mean?" And I say, "Trust me. You'll come to this realization yourself. I'm just telling you." [Then] 15 months later they come back and they say, "I had this nagging feeling you were right, but I thought that we had locked arms and done it." And I say, "I get it. You're going to have to figure out how to make this transition."

Any last words of advice for an early-stage team in terms of what they need to do to both bring in capital and scale their business?

I think from a team perspective, do not compromise on the quality of people for the sake of expediency. You obviously have to move quickly when you're a small team, but somebody who's a great cultural fit and enthusiastic, but not talented enough, that doesn't work. And someone who's super talented but will come in and just spread small amounts of poison, that's not helpful either, right? And there's such a premium on speed today and sense of urgency around execution, which is totally justified. The best teams to figure out how to execute super-fast, but not giving in on the quality of people they bring in or building out the culture and the way they work together.

Your First Few Hires

Outside of the founding team, the first few hires in any startup can make or break the success of the company. They often work as hard or harder than the founders. They take on multitudes of tasks and roles, wearing many hats; they deal with massive amounts of uncertainty and change. They just get stuff done because there is so much to do and simply not enough money or people to do it.

Who They Are

The first few hires in a startup need to be hearty souls who simply <u>believe</u> in you and in the mission. These people 'walk across hot coals for <u>you</u> and your co-founders, because they see the opportunity on the other side.

The roles filled by these first few hires depend a lot on the composition of your founding team and the state of your new product. Often, they are engineers or product developers because the product isn't quite done, or it isn't done enough to be ready for prime time. If they are engineers, they will take on far more "product management" tasks than they would in a more mature company. They will define key features, speak to customers, set the language and tone of the description of the functionality, produce analytics of usage and customer behavior, and answer support tickets.

You will likely be adding early-stage product managers and product developers who have the creativity to try new things, the persistence to handle repeated failures, and the adaptability to manage ever-changing priorities and job requirements.

As the product matures, you will also be hiring a marketing or sales person, or perhaps both, to assist the founding team in selling.

In terms of seniority, these roles are usually mid-level rather than executive or junior-level. Executives often won't, or can't, do the grunt work, while junior staff often need a great deal of guidance to know where to head. While this is not universally the case, either situation will take a lot of time for you as a founder. There is no hard-and-fast rule, but mid-level professionals are both capable of setting direction, *and* actually doing the work.

What They Will Do

At this stage, you should probably define roles for every new hire but also keep a significant amount of flexibility. Your exact product, business model, go-to-market approach, and organizational structure are all experimental; they will change, and your company will change, sometimes significantly.

If they are marketing folks, they will do some elements of demand generation, corporate marketing, product marketing, customer training, sales training, and product management.

If they are software developers, they will do front-end and back-end work, design specifications, debugging, and speaking with customers. The point is that any functional role will be broad and varied, and far outside the norm of a larger business. One founder, Edith Harbaugh (interview later in the book) said that everyone had to fold T-shirts for a meetup they were having. You pretty much cannot have people say "that is not my job" in an early-stage startup.

How to Approach Hiring Your Early Employees

Hiring these early employees is very different from hiring at scale, because these employees need to embrace the many hats rather than chafe against them. At the early stage, you have very little evidence that your business will be successful for the prospective employee to evaluate. You can tell them how great the company will be, but you don't have much to stand behind. You probably don't have many great customers, lots of revenue, much capital, or even a stable product. Your two certainties are uncertainty and opportunity.

Due to the uncertainty, the employee is coming on board based on the passion and salesmanship of the CEO or other founder they will work for. You and your co-founders need to do a lot of selling to these early employees. The employee needs to like you, believe in you, and love your mission.

Alongside the necessary skills, you are equally looking for specific traits that are necessary and non-negotiable assets:

1. Open-minded attitude and a willingness to take on all the varied tasks

2. Comfort with change. The company's focus, the product, the business model, and their role will all change significantly on a monthly and annual basis.

3. Resiliency. Startups are really difficult—bad news, tough times, and bumps in the road are commonplace. You need people who know how to get up from the dirt, dust themselves off, and start a new day or new project alongside other team members.

4. Hunger to learn. This doesn't just mean learning new skills, but also learning and evaluating *what didn't work* so they can try a new way next time.

This type of resiliency is less about "eternal optimism" and more about a constant sense of pragmatism and moving forward. You want the person who can say, "Wow, that news yesterday really sucked and was a huge setback. Now what are we going to do about it? What is our plan going forward, and what are we going to work on _today_?"

A hunger to learn is also critical because inevitably, these early employees will have to take on tasks that are well beyond their current scope of knowledge. They might need to go much deeper inside their own function, like a content marketer who needs to learn about PR or email marketing, or take on elements of a function that is well beyond their current skill or understanding.

A good example of this is an engineer who needs to take on elements of customer support. If the product is buggy, or needs crucial functions, the engineering team needs to directly dialogue with the customers to get the product right. No one says engineers are customer support experts. But engineers who don't want to talk directly with customers won't help an early stage technology business really nail the product.

You are looking for the best available athlete, not an all-star point guard. These athletes should have a broad set of skills, but more importantly, a willingness and ability to learn the skills they don't have.

Even more, they have to do what needs doing _without a support team_ and _without complaining about it_. People who won't wash out the coffee cups or book their own travel, or any number of other tasks, won't cut it.

What's interesting is that the need to wear so many hats generally changes over time. It's not the personal resilience or the willingness to pitch in that changes. As the company grows, you will move from a "generalist" to more of a "specialist" model. People will either adapt or leave the business.

This transition is an important one. Many of the CEOs interviewed, such as Rob Chesney, Amy Errett, and Steve Hafner, discuss it. It also relates to the hiring of team leads and executives, who will tend to be more "specialized" in their functions.

Kevin O'Brien, co-Founder and CEO of security company GreatHorn, put it well in a LinkedIn essay. O'Brien believes that hiring an amazing team is the CEO's most important job[2].

"...the single most important thing that the CEO can do is find, hire, and retain absolutely incredible people. It's astonishing how many problems you can outrun if you have incredibly smart people dealing with real problems around you; bringing them together is also one of the hardest things you'll do."

The first few team members that you hire will be absolutely critical to the success of your startup. They are almost founder-like in their passion and belief in the mission and in their importance to the culture. Choose wisely, and over-emphasize values and work ethic over skills at this point. If possible, choose people with strong networks who will, themselves, attract great people.

Read on to see how other successful founders have done this.

---

[2] LinkedIn post - https://www.linkedin.com/pulse/startup-ceos-most-important-job-building-amazing-team-kevin-o-brien/

Interview with Edith Harbaugh, Founder & CEO, LaunchDarkly

Edith Harbaugh is the founder and CEO of LaunchDarkly, a SaaS business that serves software developers. She previously ran product management for TripIt (acquired by Concur), Monster, and Vignette.

Rob Kornblum:
Tell me a little bit about the founding of LaunchDarkly. How many co-founders did you have? How well did you know them and how well did you know you were going to work together?

Edith Harbaugh:
I've known my co-founder John since college. We stayed friends after I started working and he was getting his PhD. I think it was 2004 that we [said we] should start a company together some day. Finally, in 2012 or 2013 I said, "Look, let's start working on any idea about 10 hours a week."

So, we kept our day jobs, and we just started working on ideas for 10 hours. The first three ideas just kind of went nowhere, but we still liked working together. Then finally we had the right idea, and we quit our jobs and started working full time on it.

Were you also testing for compatibility?

Oh yeah. I said, "Hey, let's try working together 10 hours a week and see if this is happening. If it turns out that we don't work too well together, that's fine. We can still be friends." Yeah, I think that actually helped.

How long did that phase last, testing ideas and each other?

About a year and a half to two years. We had careers that were going quite well, so we were really waiting for the right idea.

In that compatibility testing phase, how did you know you would work well together? On the skills side, what were you looking for to kind of round out your own skills?

I had gone much more down the business path in product management and marketing, and I didn't really know that if he was a good coder or not. (He'd get offended if he heard me say that.) Fortunately, John is absolutely brilliant and a really good manager, and just the sharpest guy, but you don't really know that until you work together.

Obviously the startup journey is pretty bumpy. Were you looking for resilience, or just an understanding of how best to hire...all the other pieces that you need as a founder?

Yeah, we talked through what kind of customers we wanted to have. When we reached the end of an idea, we would talk through whether or not it was the end. One of the ideas we worked on a long time was the productization of his thesis. [After about a year] I just finally said 'I don't think this idea's going anywhere, I'm really sorry." And he's like, "Yeah, I came to the same realization. Let's move on." I thought it was going to be really contentious, but he had this pragmatic way of looking at life.

Instead of saying the year was wasted, we both said, "We learned a lot. Let's move on to the next idea." Which was the lens of somebody I wanted to work with, that you're always learning more, not, "Let's keep going on a bad idea for forever."

You've raised a fair bit of capital. At what point did you turn to investors? Was it just the two of you, or had you rounded out the team further?

In hindsight, it seems crazy. He was making... a ton of money. I persuaded him to quit and we bootstrapped it. So we were living off our savings, and then John said he has this absolutely wonderful engineer who he'd worked with before that he really wanted to hire (we had no money). So we scraped together $8,000, and we said to the engineer that we would pay him for a month while I would go out and fundraise. So that's why we originally fundraised, to start hiring engineers.

What were the investor interactions with you and John? What were their recommendations in terms of building out the rest of the team?

It was super early stage, so...Basically, everybody turned us down. The only people who said yes were people who had worked with John and me before. So, the original investors were my old bosses from TripIt and Vignette, and John's old bosses. Everybody who did not know us were like, "We don't understand what they're doing. This is going nowhere." But our original investors told me later they had [thought], "We had no idea what we were doing, but we knew that you would do something [good]."

At Military.com, I'd taken it from about $10 million to $50 million in about a year; I did the same at TripIt. It was funny, because a lot of people who'd honestly never invested before, [they] just really wanted to be part of it.

As you moved past hiring people you knew, tell me about how that went. How did you sell them on the opportunity? [Offer some] advice for other early stage founders who are in that phase.

Hiring is super hard. We would post on AngelList, because we were still a super risky, early-stage company...then we raised $2 million. So we did have some money. Enough to pay people, like our designer from an AngelList ad. Our first marketing hire was circulating her resumé to startups that we knew [were] looking for jobs.

Did you do anything to differentiate your opportunity from others, besides getting them excited? How much of that did you do personally?

It was really high-touch back then. If I knew somebody was interested, I would personally call them, get coffee, tell them about how they would have this huge ground-floor opportunity to make a difference, and make the offer. We didn't have an HR person.

What were the cultural elements that you were trying to hire for? How did you go about trying to screen for those?

My comparison back then was it was like being on a submarine. When we were four people, part of our culture was eating all our meals together at lunch. If somebody wanted to go get coffee, they would say, "Does anybody else want to go get coffee?" We very much moved as a pack.

When we were interviewing somebody new, they would come eat a meal with us. I would tell them up front, "Hey, if you come work here, you're going to be hanging out with us...during work hours, nine hours a day, so this better suit you." That was definitely part of our interview.

You'd been pretty successful in the past, so what other things did you take from those experiences into startup recruiting?

At the really early stage, what I discovered is, I hate it when somebody hands me the manual. I would like to figure it out myself. Some people want the manual handed to them, and they should not be in a five-person startup.

I'd discover the person's notion of a startup by asking, "What's the smallest company you've been at, and what did you like or dislike about it?" When they thought of a startup, they thought of something that was more like a 30-person or 300-person company. But when you're a five-person company, it was all our job. When we did a Meetup, we all folded t-shirts.

How did you try to screen in or screen out people who are OK with that?

I would absolutely ask [if they] would mind answering support tickets. If they said, "That's really not my job," then I know it isn't going to work. Answering support tickets is a pretty good filter.

I had been in eight or nine-person startups before, and the engineers had a terrible attitude. Everything was not their job. We had a separate support person. And I just knew that I didn't want to build that culture again.

As you guys went from that [five-person group], three-and-a-half years ago to the next phase... to 20, 25 people. Was your approach to hiring different in terms of either the person [or] the screening process?

We were eight people when we closed our A round. We had made that $2 million last about as long as I could. We eked it out for two years, and then we started actually selling a lot, and then I could go get an A round of $8.7 million dollars, enough to staff up.

The way we ran the company when we were eight people was very different. We had a daily standup. Because if you're eight people, you just go around the room, like, "What are you working on today?" After we raised our A, I told the team, " Bear with us while we work out some of the kinks. Everything we did to get us to now is awesome, but we're going to have to do it differently to get us to the next stage."

We started to hire more specialists. We hired our first VP of Sales. We were still trying to screen, though, for people that were self-starters. We actually wrote down our values, which we hadn't done before.

My co-founder and I both kind of looked at values as a thing that hangs on the wall that nobody looks at, but later I said,

"When we start hiring two to three people a month, we can't just expect them to learn by osmosis, hanging out and seeing the way we do things. More than that, they're going to outnumber us. We need to figure out what we want them to know about our culture [and our values], so they learn it very quickly."

We did a survey of our team at that time, they had real examples of things that we had done in the past that they liked...I actually now give [the speech], especially the new hires, about "These are our values and where they came from." Which is all stuff that we just had not done when we were a small team.

How do you try to reinforce those values throughout the year and throughout the years as you grow?

When there is something that we feel is part of our values, we'll call it out. When I give feedback to the leadership team, I'll say, "Hey, this thing that you're doing is not really in accordance with our values." So I try to invoke praise and also when it's not really the way it should be.

How much time do you, personally, or you and co-founder spend hiring right now, since you guys are a bit bigger?

When we did our annual, we were at about 20 people, and when we were getting our Series B together, I really needed to build out a leadership team. We hired a new finance director, we hired a customer success director, we hired a VP of engineering. Now at 40 people, I'm trying to hire a VP of Marketing. We are trying to move from being a two-person show [me and my co-founder] to an actual company.

So in that flurry, how much time were you spending on hiring?

It felt like 80% because I was trying to fill three simultaneous roles.

Was that predominantly through your network, through your VCs, recruiters? What tools were you using for that?

We used anything we could to get the word out, but definitely used recruiters at this stage, because we could afford them.

Do you have best practices for startups on working with recruiters?

A recruiter is the face of your company. We almost lost a hire because he hated the recruiter. He did join us, and he said, "Well, I really liked you. It's just, I could see past the recruiter." Really pay attention to that.

The recruiter is the [candidate's] perception of your company. So this recruiter was giving really heavy-handed sales to the hire, like, "Oh, you need to make up your mind or she's going to pull the offer," which is not my style at all. You need to give a decision within a week, but I'm not going to give you 24 hours to make a major decision. So I fired the recruiter.

How have you best promoted your own values and culture through the recruiter to the candidates?

We have other recruiters now. A lot of the team has families, so we don't really do happy hour or dinners. I said to the recruiters, "When you come and eat lunch, you get a feel for the company." To eat lunch with us is to understand us.

It's nothing extravagant, but I think it makes people form tighter bonds if they actually sit down and eat. It prevents the company from fracturing, because it's hard to bear a grudge if you sit next to somebody. And it also cuts down on meetings. "Hey, let's talk about it over lunch."

So that's something you reinforce. Does the whole company do that?

Yeah, every day. We don't have one discussion going, because now we're too big, but everybody sits down at these big lunch tables.

Cool. What are some of the things that come through that are unique?

We're not super hierarchical or cliquey. Respect for each other is one of our values, so having an opportunity to get together makes people respect each other. Like I said, we're recruiting a VP of marketing; he said after eating lunch with us that we were his top pick, because we have fun. And not fun in a Nerf gun, shot-gunning beer-type way, but like, "Hey, we hang out and we make jokes together." We have camaraderie.

I think a lot of people have taken the catered food, and the games, and a bunch of other things which are symbols, [not] culture. Culture is how you ... can joke together and you show respect for each other; your value is [to] all sit down and be together.

Yeah. Along those lines, a deliberate decision we made was we don't have a ping-pong table or foosball table. My co-founder and our first engineer have two kids, and they kind of want to get their work done and go home. We do have board games, which is a big part of us.

I deliberately try not to write to people off-hours unless it's an emergency. Sometimes I'll write out an email but not press send, because I don't want to have this expectation that just because the CEO wrote you at 10:00 p.m. that you have to respond. I would like to save that for the time when I actually do really want you to respond.

I want people to bring their best self to work, and then go home. One of our deliberate values is having a hobby, whether it's children or bicycling, but something that is not work to keep you kind of sane. In interviews, I get a sense of people and ask, "What do you do that's important to you?"

How do you think about continuing that communication throughout a bigger team? Is there a point at which you are a little nervous, from a size perspective?

If you're not a little nervous, you're not doing a startup. Your culture is as good as the last person you hire. I'm always nervous. All I can do is try and reinforce with the leadership team the way I want the company to behave and be there.

Do you still interview everyone?

I do not. No matter what the role, there's one person whose job it is just to interview for values. For example, if it's an engineer, they'll have the technical side, but then somebody will come in and just do a half hour on [whether] we think this person is compatible with our values.

We haven't had somebody who's a really bad value fit yet. I also do a lot of reference checking...People can sometimes fake an interview, but references are usually good about getting the real side. We have had to let a couple people go for performance, which is always painful.

At this point, you've been able to screen out the values misfits.

Yeah, and I know that it's just a matter of time until it happens... Nobody's infallible. But it has not happened yet.

How have the internal systems grown? Did you codify them, and how did you go about instituting that?

Now we do formal onboarding, so after we ask interviewees what they want to do, every manager writes up a 30, 60, or 90-

day plan to review with new employees, which I got from Anne Dwane [Edith's former manager at Military.com]. She did that for me when I joined, so I feel like I got the benefit of a Harvard Business School education without the tuition.

I really look at any time getting up to speed as basically a dead cost. I don't believe in the wasteful [school of] Hire People and Let Them Figure It Out. Objectives [can be broad, but tasks should be clear]. For example, we just hired a customer success person. We had not had customer success before but, "Okay, figure out what customer success means at our company. Be ready on this date to present it to the team." For somebody more junior, like a salesperson, it'll be much more specific.

And the onboarding piece obviously has a goal of getting up to speed. Presumably, it also has a "getting to know us", how we work, where to turn, etc.

Something I like doing... are all-hands [meetings every two weeks]. I introduce new people, any important messages, get people reinforced about the vision, and kind of get everybody back together. "Monica, tell the team why you joined our company." This gets [people] to describe in their own words what they're excited about and what they're interested in... It kind of reinforces that, "Hey, this is an exciting place to be at."

The format we've [settled] on is, we'll do a welcome, I'll talk about the vision, and then the technical team will do some sort of demo, and the sales team will give a customer spotlight of a deal they just closed. At the end we do something we call "thumbs up", which is an employee peer recognition program, where people nominate each other for an award.

Those are all really significant cultural reinforcement mechanisms. When you onboard poorly, people bounce.

Oh, yeah. And it's just debilitating for the rest of the team. One of the companies where I worked, we never had an all-hands, so nobody ever knew what was happening. Literally, somebody would join, and we'd all be whispering, "Who is that person? What do they do, can I help them?" When the founders left that company, I got a promotion to director, and I started doing all-hands as a reaction to what I don't really like about startups about new people not knowing everyone.

How are you managing communication? How are you going to change when you're at 40 to 50 people?

Yeah, on my top 20 things to think about, it's not on my horizon. We didn't do all-hands until the A round was done. On an eight-person team, everyone knows who the new person is, because we just got coffee together. I do think culture is additive.

After we closed our Series B, somebody said to me, "How are we going to make sure our culture stays exactly the same?" And I said, "We don't. Let's just make sure it changes in ways that we all want it to change."

Building an Amazing Culture

Developing a world-class culture is one of the most important jobs a CEO and founding team can take on. Your culture will define how you hire, promote, and make decisions; it defines how hard everyone works, and what you work on. It will impact the types of people who you attract to your company and whether you are able to retain them.

The right culture will enable your company to grow quickly; the wrong culture, and your company will break. If product is the body of the company, team is the oxygen and culture is the blood vessels for the oxygen. No matter how good your product is, your team and the culture you build are THE critical elements in achieving hypergrowth.

Culture, however, is not perks and benefits. The media likes to "play up" stories about startup perks and benefits. We have probably all read articles about Google's amazing cafeterias and free food, Netflix's unlimited vacation policy, or some other company's kegs on tap, etc. None of those things are culture, those are all perks, which is one *very small* element of culture.

Your company's culture is set from the top down, but it grows and takes life from the bottom up. Why do you need to establish culture from the top? It will establish itself, so it might as well be the culture you want.

Culture is the embodiment of what you value, how you communicate, and how you operate.

Let's say you hire a superstar developer (or sales person or designer or accountant, the function doesn't matter). You determine that he is excellent at doing his job, but he does not get along with of his coworkers. There have been a few complaints about callous things he has said in meetings and people are now starting to get frustrated by his behavior.

Do you:

- Give him a bonus at the end of the year because his performance is excellent?
- Fire him because he is not a fit with his coworkers?
- Keep him on but coach him about his style?

Interestingly, there is no right answer. You *desperately* need A players who are really good, but you have a small team; you need to get along and at least respect the people you work with. If you keep him on, others may leave, or you may degrade the productivity of the rest of the group. Your decision will show your team what you value most and what your culture says about performance versus likeability and respect.

Since the people inside the company are your key recruiting tool, he will attract more people like him. Lastly, more people inside the company may start to act like this employee.

In his best-selling book *The Advantage*, author and organizational consultant Patrick Lencioni makes the case that "organizational health... is the single greatest advantage that any company can achieve."

Lencioni tends to study larger companies rather than startups, so his claim may be a little strong for a startup that is struggling to survive. After all, having a great culture but failing to create a product that customers want is not going to produce a high-value company.

But the inverse is also true—having an amazing product and a terrible culture will surely sub-optimize the outcome of a new business. Customer service and productivity will lag, turnover will increase, B and C players will be hired, and ultimately the company will not become what it could have.

Culture is a manifestation of what your company cares about, what it values.

So back to the question I posed above- there is a reason Netflix and other high-growth companies have developed a "no brilliant jerks" policy. The problem with brilliant jerks is that they destroy the performance of the team, and they hamper the ability to hire other A players. Who wants to work with jerks?

How To Develop Culture

In my previous book *Never Too Late to Startup*, I outlined a series of questions for founders who are just beginning to establish their culture. Similar to exercises I use in private workshops, they can be effective at boiling down "esoteric" concept of values to real-world experience:

> *What traits do you really value in colleagues?*
>
> *Who have been the best people you've worked with in your career? Why? What made them so good in your eyes?*
>
> *Who do you respect the most as a boss? Why? Who do you respect least? Why?*
>
> *What kinds of things are you good at and want to do more of?*
>
> *What energizes you professionally?*
>
> *What things de-energize you?*

NOTE: *If you are interested in having me work with your team to define or articulate your values, or to help you build hiring programs to support your growth, feel free to reach out to me at rob@startlaunchgrow.com*

Taking the time to answer these questions will go a long way toward outlining the culture that you want to build. Once you know what you value most, and how you want people to act toward each other, you can begin building the processes and norms that will reinforce the culture.

Sometimes I speak with early-stage entrepreneurs and when I mention "process" they push back. To them, process is a "big company" thing that they are trying to avoid. They are equating process with bureaucracy. Depending on the size and stage of the company, you can have a simplified process or a super complicated one.

But for super important tasks, like hiring people, if you don't create *some kind* of process, then people will just wing it. You will end up with very bad hires. Also, there will be little alignment between those new hires and the most important things that you need to do inside the company.

This is an example of a simplistic but good process. If you really value creativity and speed inside your company, then you should screen for and hire creative people, problem solvers who are not overly data driven. Also, you should live your culture, making sure that your hiring process is a speedy one.

Culture is not about uniformity of thought. In fact, healthy conflict is often the sign of a great culture. Intel Corporation, the legendary and now giant chip company, had a great model that they called "disagree and commit." Even when people couldn't come to agreement around a contentious issue, they were expected to speak up and get their opinions out there. Regardless of whether they agreed with the decision, they were expected to support the final decision.

Lencioni believes,

"Most people are generally reasonable and can rally around an idea that wasn't their own as long as they know they've had a chance to weigh in. But when there is no conflict, when different opinions have not been aired and debated, it becomes virtually impossible for team members to commit to a decision, at least not actively."

I believe that healthy conflict comes from wide-ranging diversity: diversity of background, gender, age, race, and experience. Many of the CEOs who were interviewed for this book cautioned against looking for "culture fit" in interviews; they believe that it results in bias against those who are "different" under the umbrella excuse of "not fitting in."

Founder Actions Establish Culture

I believe that actions are the basis of culture, and in the case of a startup, it is the actions of the founders.

Glenn Elliott and Debra Corey's book _Build It, The Rebel Playbook for World-Class Employee Engagement_ highlights that culture as:

"How your company behaves, recruits, makes decisions, operates, makes choices, through the actions of your leaders and managers".

Elliott and Corey believe that having a clear mission is the key to driving the behavior:

"A well-developed, clearly articulated and inspiring mission will:

• Give employees something bigger and more meaningful to work toward, which has proven positive impact on results

- Let customers connect with you on a deeper level
- Support long-term decision-making, aligning everyone with a clear common goal"

I interviewed David Mandell, founder and CEO of PivotDesk, for my last book *Never Too Late to Startup*. He described their culture to me this way:

> "I think the single most important attribute that not only I look for in employees... is respect. And respect for everyone in the organization. The second that people don't show respect for others, or people don't deserve respect from others, we have to make changes. A lot of people think culture is based on foosball tables and catered lunches and that's all bullshit. What you need is an organization that enjoys working together, because that's when they work best together.
>
> And the first step in an organization that enjoys working together is mutual respect. I mean that at every level of the organization, so... being a senior person does not in any way give you the right to be disrespectful to a junior person. Everyone that is here is here because they are really good at what they do. Some may have a lot more experience than others, but they're all really good people, and they are all critical to our success. And the second anyone in our organization shows lack of respect I virtually stop everything and we either fix it or we make a change."

I believe it is also critically important to describe not only the values you want, but also the behaviors that you expect will embody those values. Slack, one of the fastest growing software companies in history, does this well. Its leaders not only laid out their values of "Diligence, Curiosity, and Empathy" but then described what those meant:

"Diligence: We know that the success of our product will likely not come from unpredictable lightning strikes but from grinding hard rocks against other hard rocks day after day. To build a product that works well and is magical comes out of effort that looks very non-magical. It is easy and sometimes tempting to say "good enough" but after this is where the best work happens and what makes Slack special. This is also where your best work happens.

Curiosity: We are building something that most people don't know they need. Every day, we are venturing into unknown territory. Thriving at Slack means recognizing this forward position and that you may not know the best direction to head. This means you ask good questions at the right time to the right people. It means being curious about how things work and what our customers need. Curiosity is not being satisfied with the status quo and looking at every problem deeper and from a multitude of angles.

Empathy: Building things for others to use is an act of empathy. Every decision made about how a thing is built and how it should be used comes from the worldview of the maker. How well they can see things through the user's eyes determines the value of their work. No one person can see the world through another's eyes. It's all approximation and guesswork. Thus, the only way for us to broaden our understanding of our users, to see things the way they do, is through hiring people with as many diverse experiences and backgrounds as we can."

Don't be afraid to do a little inventory of the qualities you're looking for in hires. I don't simply mean skills, but values, family, personality, and style. Think about, articulate, and write down those qualities you're trying to build in your startup.

Like Mandell, I met Lew Cirne, an incredibly successful software entrepreneur, for my last book. When he founded his second company, New Relic, he was in a different stage of life than with his earlier company. He thoughtfully built New Relic's culture to reflect these changes. (I believe the team and culture are a huge factor in New Relic's success. It is now a multi-billion dollar public company).

> "I want New Relic employees to love their Mondays. I use that term all the time. I ask people, "Do you love your Mondays?" And I happen to love my Mondays. I think it's an important way to think about it. [There are] two fundamental reasons why I love my Mondays and [why] I want New Relic employees to love their Mondays: One is you love the work you do, you feel like it matters and it has impact and it gives you joy. And [two is] you love the people you work with. They bring out the best in you and they encourage you and they help you grow.

> When I started the company before I had a Series A [funding], the kind of ground rules I had was we're going to look for a more experienced employee base, capable of doing more in a shorter period of time, and is less likely to burn out. We're going to have a standard minimum three-week vacation policy. We're going to encourage people to take all of it and not store it up. [A] two-week vacation policy is crazy in my mind. You need three weeks of vacation every year... where you are really disconnecting so that you can really recharge.

> The other thing I thoughtfully put into the culture is I make a habit of leaving the office at 5:00 every night because one of the important things to me is

dinner with the family, and I like to cook the dinner... it is just a routine I have. Certainly I want it not to be, 'Oh, Lew the founder gets away with it,' [so] it's a pretty quiet office between 5:00 and 5:30 at New Relic, compared to most other high-growth companies."

Art Papas, founder of the highly successful software company Bullhorn, Inc., implemented a system to screen for culture during the interview process. He also applies this system to reinforce the culture during the company's annual reviews and bonus compensation process. (I used to work at Bullhorn and reported to him.)

Papas defines his company's core values in five key phrases or behaviors:

1. Ownership
2. Energy
3. Agility and speed
4. Service
5. Being human

He and his team go further than just listing values. Along with his company's HR head and executive team, he defines what those phrases mean in terms of behavior. They use everyday examples so that employees and prospective employees know what matters and whether or not they're a good fit. For example, the team defines the value "Energy" in behavioral terms:

- Leave people positively charged.

- Build up your teammates.

- If you see a problem, present constructive feedback directly to the source.

- Act in the interest of the team.

- Accept critical feedback with an open mind.
- Make people want to work with you again.

Equally important, Papas' core values include definitions of *what not to do*, which includes the value of Energy:

- Talk behind people's backs.
- Stir the pot.

The management guru, Peter Drucker, once said, "Culture eats strategy for breakfast." Personally, I think "*team* eats strategy for breakfast" but culture is the fundamental support structure for team. Culture enables team members to gain trust and rely on each other. Culture lets team members challenge one another in a positive way, to produce the best answers for the company.

Many of the interviews in this book touch on culture, because hiring and culture are so intertwined. I encourage you as a founder to spend some time thinking about how you want to build, support, nurture, and be part of the culture you want, to enable the success you envision.

Interview with Sean Byrnes, Founder & CEO, Outlier.ai

Sean Byrnes is the founder and CEO of Outlier.ai, and a former founder of Flurry, a mobile analytics company that was acquired by Yahoo for over $200 million.

Rob Kornblum:
Sean, maybe you could start with telling me a little bit about the founding of Outlier, a little bit of the story? And then we can talk more about the team building and culture side of things.

Sean Byrnes:
I have been an entrepreneur now for about twelve years. My last company was a company called Flurry, which I started in 2005, which we grew over nine years [into] one of the largest analytics companies in the world.

Even [after] we sold it to Yahoo in 2014, [customers] started asking me a very simple question, which was, "What am I supposed to be looking for in all this data?"

And that became the founding idea of Outlier, was a complete rethinking of Business Intelligence from the ground up.

I ended up starting Outlier myself in January of 2015. My co-founder joined me in April of 2015 after a very thorough process of working together on projects to see how we worked together under stress; [he and I did] a lot of reference checking about people who had worked with us, how we operated, what was our style. And then, it culminated in a very long, epic session where I spent two-and-a-half hours trying to talk him out of it, trying to convince him Outlier was such a bad idea.

Today, our customers are large public e-commerce and media companies that are dealing with tens of millions of consumer transactions. They want to understand things as they're happening so that they can take action: when does customer behavior start changing within certain customer segments? Or when does customer demographics shift? Or revenue composition? They don't want to wait until these things snowball into big impacts on larger business.

We'll get them there early enough to actually get on the train instead of just watching it pull out of the station.

You mentioned your co-founder. So, was it just the two of you when you started?

Well, it was just me when I got started. I learned a lot in the process [of building Flurry] about founders, and specifically that it's not enough that you know somebody well and they're friends of yours. You really need to understand and work with them in a high-pressure environment, because otherwise, the things you learn and the conflicts that erupt are difficult.

I spent a lot of time coaching start-up companies that have founder issues, and almost all of them are based on bad expectation setting. So, they go in as best friends and expect that friendship will mean they work well together, or one founder wants to just build something and sell it, and the other one wants to build a billion-dollar business, and that doesn't work out. So, you need to be very thoughtful about who you bring on the team.

I've also been better this time around, since I've been down this adventure before. The short version is that the first time you ride a roller coaster, you're white-knuckled the whole time. You're scared the entire time, because you don't know when to be scared. You don't know when you're going up, when you're going down and so you're just freaking out the whole time. And that's what a first-time founder is like.

And the second time around, you actually are much more relaxed because you know when to be scared. But, when you're scared, you're more scared than you were the first time. Because you know exactly how scary it will be.

In that process of vetting, what skills or traits were you looking for to round out yourself? And how did you go about trying to find that?

Some people believe that you have to bring on co-founders that have very specific, complementary skill sets. I actually think that is less important, because the most important thing is compatibility. Is this somebody you can work with, under stress, who shares the same kind of vision, philosophy, where you can have a very transparent relationship? I can't tell you the number of founders I know that don't feel like they can share everything with their co-founders. And I think the minute that happens, your relationship has already started to devolve. So really, my goal was to find somebody I felt like I could work with very well, for a long period of time, potentially nine to 10 years of my life, in highly stressful environments and not have issues erupt along the way.

In my experience, as you're building teams, you don't draw an org chart and put people in it. You build a team out of the best people you find, and the team ends up defining itself. And so, regardless of the skill set of who we brought on board, we would eventually just bring everybody else to augment around them. It just happened to be Mike was very perfect for this particular company, which is really luck more than anything else.

How did you sell the opportunity to your first few hires who weren't founders? How did you differentiate your start-up from the lots of other start-ups, or from other bigger companies?

I believe early-stage hiring is, like I said, less about org charts and very little about roles, for example. Because in an early-stage company, the only thing that differentiates people is typically what they're focused on. There are not really roles; everybody is doing everything. And so, essentially what I did in this case, is make a list of all the different company-killing risks. And then the goal is to hire somebody whose focus is to mitigate each of those risks working your way down the line.

The biggest risk to Outlier is an existential risk, that we run out of money and don't exist. So, that's my job, as a CEO, to make sure that doesn't happen. The next risk would be, you know, we're an artificial intelligence company. If our AI doesn't work, then everything else is academic. So, that's Mike's job. His focus is on that. [Now] we have to build a product people can use on top of that data science.

And that became the first hire we made, Anthony Watkins, who had worked for me at Flurry [and] was a good friend. I hired him at Flurry to run our partner's group and then when I was getting Outlier started, he was very excited.

He had lived this problem personally and really like the idea of what we were doing. I think that a lot of those first employees are joining to work with *you*. The opportunity, the work, and the potential has to be interesting, and ours was. But at the end of the day, that's true of almost every venture-backed company that's ever raised a seed around the funding in their entire lives. Because seed investors wouldn't invest if those things weren't true.

So, after that, those first few employees are typically people that you know. [We] hired, as our head of customer development, somebody that Anthony and I knew from our graduate program, because then the next biggest risk was, 'Can we get customer feedback and start to understand the customer need better.'

And then the next company-killing risk was [that] our systems have to scale. You're talking about a lot of data from a lot of companies and so we brought on our lead engineer. He had worked for Anthony at Flurry. He was one of the top engineers at the company. At the same time, he had never run engineering before. A lot of these opportunities are really taking a bet on a person. People take a bet on your company that it'll be productive, but you also take a bet on them.

I believe that if you find people that have a fairly varied history, meaning they've done lots of different things, and learned consistently over that time, that what they're telling you is that they're students and they're adaptable. They're interested in learning and doing new things, and being challenged in new ways. They haven't done the same thing for 10 years and want to just keep doing it the same way. And those are the kinds of people that I always look for in the early stages, because you don't know what you'll be asking them to do in six months. Because the company will change radically in six months.

I think that [being challenged in new ways is] the thing that start-ups offer that big companies don't. Well, there are two things. One is you've got a bigger impact. Everything you do every day impacts the company. But also, variety. You do different things every day, and so you don't get bored showing up at work every day, doing the same thing, day after day.

Do you think about hiring differently now than you did a year ago, given that variability, when you mentioned you don't know what you're going to be doing in six months?

No, not specifically. There's a point where you can start hiring specialists, but I think that's farther down the line. I wasn't looking to take engineers and throw them into sales and vice versa. So, there was definitely a limit to how much I was looking for outside of the focus.

But again, we're still not hiring for role. And so, if you join us as a sales leader, you're also doing marketing because we need to generate leads. You're also doing customer service because we don't have a huge customer success team...your focus is going to be on selling and everything else becomes secondary to that. And that model worked very well at Flurry.

Again, going back to my original philosophy that company teams are essentially built out of the best people you find, not out of the people you want. It's interesting how the life and trajectory of companies changes with those people who find you.

I have a firm belief that your ability to succeed as a start-up company is directly proportional to the adaptability of your team, because the only guarantee you have is constant change. And if your team cannot thrive in a world of constant change, then you won't thrive and you won't succeed.

That's the goal with Outlier as well. I don't know what the next few years hold with Outlier. I can tell you that the world is different now than when I got started in 2015, and will be different in three years, but I don't know how it will be different or how we'll have to change. But I have a very adaptable team that I know will be able to adjust and thrive in that world.

You mentioned you're about to double the team, including a couple of senior hires. How much time do you personally spend on hiring?

Oh, in the early days, I think that you should spend all your time hiring. There's nothing more than investing in your team. When I'm not selling, I'm hiring. I don't really do anything else. I would love to spend 100% of my time hiring, which I plan to do the minute that we do have somebody who can sell and I'm not the only salesperson.

And within that, on a weekly basis, are you thinking more about pipeline?

If you put yourself on a deadline, hiring never works out very well. And so the biggest challenge in being the founder and the CEO is having the, for lack of a better term, intestinal fortitude to wait for the right person. It's hard to be patient and thorough. It's easy to panic and just hire somebody just because you need somebody right then, [for an acute need]. It never works out well. You build teams to the best people and you need to find people that you are excited to join your team. If you're not excited about...adding them to your team will meaningfully increase the value of your company, then you haven't found the right person yet. It's just that simple. And [theoretically] it may take you years to find the right people.

At Flurry, it took me nine months to find a VP of Marketing, and he ended up being fantastic. But nine months is a long time, and that whole time the board was very unhappy about the fact that we didn't have a VP of Marketing. And it's hard to hold the line and wait for the right person, instead of just having a person that's pretty good in the job. But it's the difference between success and failure.

On the flip side, there's some companies that can't afford to wait. You run out of money or run out of runway by the time you find the right person.

So, there's a point when you just need help. You can't do it yourself. [Now that we're] looking for a VP of Sales, search firms are helping me with the search. It needs to be someone's full-time job to find those candidates and my job to interview them and close them when we find the right ones.

Tell me how you think about culture and fit. What are the fit elements that you're trying to hire for and how do you go about screening for those?

[Honestly,] I think that "fit" is code word for bias in almost any company I've ever seen. And I think that is why it's been so difficult for women and people of color to penetrate [the] technology [industry], is that fit becomes an excuse to choose people that think like me or look like me. If you have a bunch of people with the same life experience, the same experience in their professional lives, you're going to have a lot of group think. You're not going to challenge a lot of assumptions.

And so, that's not my philosophy. I believe a corporate culture arises out of the people you hire, it's not something you create.

And I specifically like to seek out people [who] will challenge and think in new ways. All the research shows that diversity is an enormous advantage in building teams. Diversity brings a lot of different natural perspectives, and thought processes, and ideas that make and challenge your existing thought process. And so I strive to having as much diversity as I possibly can in the process.

At Outlier, our policy is that we cannot hire for any position, unless a woman has made it to the last round of the process, essentially to force ourselves out of bad habits. Does that mean we have to hire women for every position? No. But it means that I do not feel we have looked hard enough, and talked to enough people, if we had not had a woman to reach the last round of that process. Especially in engineering, where there are probably fewer female candidates that you would easily find on LinkedIn, you just have to look harder.

And that goes for all sorts of access and diversity, in terms of background, and who they are, and their life experience, and things they've seen. It goes for age diversity. You don't want a team of just twenty-something year-olds who haven't seen economic cycles. You don't want to have a team of people who all grew up in the same place, and went to the same schools, and studied the same things.

And the biggest challenge, [the exact opposite of what you want,] is that most interview processes are essentially these very sophisticated bias reinforcers, where they're designed to select people that look like the people who are already on the team.

[Outlier's] interview process is really just a job simulation. We give you a problem that is very typical for the job that you'll have, and you send us in a written solution. For developers, that might be design or code. For a customer success manager, it may be an engagement or deployment plan. For product manager, it might be a product roll-out plan. And then when you come in to visit us, the day becomes essentially a simulation as if you were an employee with that job at the company, talking about the work that you proposed, and poking holes in it, and challenging it, and talking about it.

We have a group [meeting and] then you have individual one-on-ones, and at the end of the day, you've tested about how they would do in the job if they had it. And usually everybody walks away with a very strong sense of whether or not they would do a good job [and] want to do the job. [That] is the only process I have found, personally, that is predictive of success [with the added benefit of not reinforcing any bias.] Every other interview process that I've ever seen has almost no correlation, if not negative correlation, with eventual success in a job.

We are not prescriptive in how you solve the problem we give you. [Some] people use PowerPoint slides, because they think visually. Some people write up documents, because they think in words. Some people put together spreadsheets, because they think in numbers.

Are there cultural elements that you look for or try to reinforce in your hires, in terms of personal characteristics, outside of the skill and how people will do if they have the job?

We look for people [who] want to learn...At Flurry, for example, we were a big data mobile company. I ran product and engineering which was like 70, 80 people. Almost no one we hired had any big data or mobile experience before we hired them. And they essentially learned everything they learned at the company.

Because what I found was, if you are a person [with a history of challenging yourself to learn new things], you are A) very adaptable, so you'll deal well with change, B) you want to work with a team, because by definition you're going to have to learn from them, and then you'll have to teach the next group, and so you're very team and collaboration-oriented. You find people who want to learn, but also want to teach, which is great.

But you also find people who are humble enough to realize that they're coming in not as the leader. They are going to have to work their way up and put effort in. It's not going to come easily to them, and they want a challenge, they want that effort. So, that's as close to filtering for culture that I'll do.

Humble, learners, teachers. Those are cultural elements that you try to look for and reinforce?

Many of [those who push themselves to learn new things], frankly, aren't humble. But it's okay to have a lot of self-confidence, as long as it doesn't get in the way of the collaboration element and everything else that is happening. That's why I don't go any further in the cultural filtering, because in many cases this will mean you have a team of people who are a combination of self-motivating, self-confident people.

And that's part of why I'm not prescriptive about these things is that it would be impossible for me to quantify all the different ways that people are different...so I don't even try. I basically decide then, I will bring in a team of people who want to do the work, want to learn, and want to collaborate. And the culture of the company will be defined by those people as they join.

That's really interesting. Are there elements of culture or values that you try to reinforce once people are in, through promotion mechanisms, bonus mechanisms, [or] other non-financial processes? In terms of whether that's values or culture that you, as the CEO, say are important?

For example, the company sets out the things that it values: promotion, bonus, etc. Are there elements that you're trying to reinforce?

Not in the way you're describing it. I have some common beliefs, one of which is that if there are any jackasses on your team, your hiring process has already failed. If you can't head that off, there's probably very little hope of turning around your team, because there's also some other things that made it through that are more subtle and harder to find.

I believe very firmly [that] everybody [should] know exactly how we're doing at all times because I hated working at companies where you didn't know what was happening. So, Flurry was radically transparent. Outlier is as well. Everyone at the company knows everything that's going on. There's no secrets.

I try to promote that culture of transparency, so people share everything they're doing [and you don't get surprised]. Not just what they're doing, but what they're feeling about it, when they're stressed about it, when they're challenged, so that there aren't surprises. [A failure of leadership is when] somebody comes to you and says they've been really stressed about something for a month. And you're like, "Wow, I had no idea."

At Outlier today, not on purpose, but just as things go, it turns out a lot of our employees are parents with kids. Having a culture that's focused on work-life balance is very appealing to people who have kids, who don't want to work twelve hours a day, seven days a week. So, typically what that means is that people will drop their kids off at school and come to work, usually first thing in the morning. Then they get a lot of work done before they go pick their kids up from school. So, there's not any foosball and there's no ping-pong. People are really focused, because you have a daily deadline. Then you go home, give your kids dinner, have some time, they go down to bed, you sign online and do some more work during the night. We try to minimize weekend work.

And, you know, there [are] times when that's not possible, when there's really crunch time, and big customers, and fires that are happening. But, that's the goal of what we're trying to build [as a sustainable environment]...frankly, as far as I can tell, we are more productive at Outlier with a team of eight people than I was at a team at Flurry with twice the people working crazy hours. Because you're much more thoughtful about what you do, you're thoughtful about where you spend your time, and people can be more creative because they don't constantly feel under pressure. And all the research out there shows you that the number of hours you work is completely disconnected to your productivity. And in fact, there's really a lot of reward of working less hours and being more productive.

Lew Cirne, by the way, said exactly the same thing in founding New Relic. About really valuing personal time, wanting to be an amazing work experience, but also giving people time outside the office to recharge and do the things that people need to do.

And I will tell you, it's definitely a recruiting advantage when people learn about how transparent we are and our balance. It does help us close people we probably wouldn't otherwise be able to close.

We run Outlier the way we run it because I believe that life is too short to do it otherwise. So, if you want to run your company this way, you're doing it because you believe that's the right thing to do. Simon Khalaf, who I hired as the CEO at Flurry, had this great saying, "Success is the best deodorant that you can have." And it's really true.

Well, you did say it helps you close people you might not otherwise be able to close, right?

Yeah, I'm not in any way trying to undermine everything else that I've said, it's just the reality is there are teams built in very different ways than what I'm describing that have lower standards for people, that'll hire and fire people constantly, that will be toxic places to work, that generate billions of dollars in returns. And there are companies like Outlier that are very well-designed, that have great team composition, that fail.

If you're running your company this way, it's because you choose [it as] the right thing to do. And in retrospect, I hope (and this is part of why it's important to me to run Outlier this way) that we will be a data point in a data set that will prove in

10, 20 years, that this is the better way to produce economic value.

Yeah, multi-time CEOs, we get pretty cynical. So, you start to list the few things that do seem to work very well, and hopefully you stick with those. But that list starts getting shorter and shorter the longer you do this.

I think treating people as people [is critical]. One of the things we do at Outlier, and I did this at Flurry too, is that you aren't allowed to refer to a person as a resource. Because in a previous life, when I used to work at Verizon, every person was referred to as a resource. It doesn't sound like a big deal, because it makes a lot of sense, like, "Do we have resources for this project?" Maybe you've heard of somebody's time and somebody else's time and thinking resources, [it] makes a lot of sense.

But, what I find is that it actually, in a very subtle way, starts to dehumanize your people. Like a person has a family, they have stresses outside their job that affects their job, they have needs, and wants, and goals. They aren't just a number of hours a week that you can allocate to a project. And so, by banning the word resource to refer to people, you're forced to talk about people by their names, or by what you know about them, which forces you to think about them as people, which is creating an environment where you treat people with respect. I was most proud of Flurry that we had almost no employee attrition for most of the life of the company...in a market where there was a lot of money out there, trying to lure people away. We had an environment that was very respectful, very welcoming, and that people wanted to work at.

I have an interesting yardstick to decide if your interview process is working well. Your interview process should both evaluate employees...but also expose who your company is. [You] know you're doing it right when you have candidates that you reject [who] refer their friends to you. Because, essentially what you've done is created such a clear communication of your values as a company, you've also made it seem so desirable, that somebody who didn't get through, still wants their friends to have the opportunity that they didn't necessarily get.

That's a great metric. As you scale, what are some of the things that you concern yourself with in terms of communication? What are some of the things you think about in terms of internal communication? What are some of the tools you use to make sure that things are scaling the way you want, and communication happens the way you want?

There's three ways to think about communication, I think these are important. The rest [is] around team building, just general philosophical management aspects.

One is transparency is the best policy, but just being transparent by posting everything on Wiki or Google Docs isn't good enough. You cannot assume that just because you shared something, everybody understood, and acknowledged, and really went through it. So, over-communication is critical, which means you don't just repeat things in the same meeting, but bring them up again and again, encourage people to understand how important something is, lead your team by example. Otherwise, you have the illusion of communication. People don't read it, because they don't know to, or it's not important, or they're busy.

Second, realize that lots of people communicate in different ways. Just on our customer success team at Outlier, we have people who communicate visually, they think a lot about the design and the visual representation. We have people who think very much in text, and like to write out large documents that the visual people don't read the entirety of, because they're just too long. And then we have people who communicate in wanting to have a meeting, discuss it face-to-face. None of those styles are better or worse that the others, they're just very different.

Third, you don't just communicate for the sake of communicating. You can just literally drown people in communication and information. A lot of companies and founders I know, are trying to pull back on using Slack, because

Slack has devolved into communication about the company, but also communication about fantasy football league; [basically it's] so much communication that it adversely affects productivity. It's an interesting side effect of facilitating communication that you can actually take away from company productivity, instead of continuing to contribute to it.

For example, we do a weekly all-hands meeting where we talk about what we're working on, how we feel about it, what we're worried and stressed about, and thank people for the work that they've done. And everybody knows it's happening once a week, so you don't have a lot of interrupts during the week about complaining about those things, because we know it'll happen at least every week.

And then we have twice a week demos of new product features, which means that I don't have to make time every day to look through the new feature releases. So, being proactive in creating forums for communication is important because it means that you can structure it and keep it from erupting.

There's a lot of things that organic growth can create very well, but one thing it does not create very well is communication channels...

Got it. So, are there any other [aspects of culture] that you think about, in terms of scaling, besides that communication piece? Whether that's org structure, or any other pieces that are on your mind?

Again, I think more in terms of people's focus than goals...even as we got bigger [at Flurry], the goal was always to have smaller teams of people who had a clear focus, because I find that focus, and the responsibility, and empowerment that come with it, is really important to keep smart people motivated long-term. Smart people get very unmotivated when they feel like they're a cog in a machine. But, if you empower them and give them the responsibility to own something, that is the best motivation. That is far better than any monetary motivation I've ever found, is that people want responsibility, they want to own something, and the more that that's there, the more motivated they can be.

Yeah, I totally agree with you. I've always felt like nothing happens unless somebody wakes up thinking about it.

Exactly, which goes back to one of my original hiring philosophies, is you always pick a company-killing risk and somebody's focus is on it, and that gives them clarity.

And a lot of companies have a fundamental breakdown in communication because they don't evolve, they don't realize how much they were relying on organic, informal communication, and they don't realize they have to up-level to more formal, structured communication.

But, you also can't start with structured methods because they're inefficient and not appropriate. [As] you go through these inflection points, evolve the structure of your communications, and make sure that everybody is still educated in the same way as to what they're doing.

How to Develop a Hiring Brand

Most successful startups go through growth patterns that are pretty predictable. The first five to 10 employees are often people that the founders have worked with before, or they are very well known and referenced.

Beyond that number, the startup will add people who don't know the founders and current employees. They won't really understand the mission yet.

What is Employer Branding?

It's easy to misunderstand what is meant by the concept of "employer branding." Some people think of an employer brand as the job postings and recruitment ads that your company puts out to job seekers. Others think that it means a huge and expensive marketing effort.

Employer branding is the reputation of an organization and the message that your company conveys to employees and prospective employees.

In other words, an employer brand is what you represent to people who might come work for your startup. Prospective candidates have lots of choices these days. Why do they want to come work for you?

- Belief in the mission
- Belief in the culture
- A chance for promotion and advancement
- Other people they will work with
- A chance to get rich when your startup hits it big

For many prospective employees, all of these will come into play.

Why You Need an Employer Brand

The most important questions to ask yourself are these:

- How do new prospective employees find out about my startup?
- What do I want them to discover about us?

Obviously, as a founder you are in love with the idea of your company and its mission, but prospective employees don't know any of that. Long before they step foot in the door, you need to communicate that mission to them, and your excitement.

In this transparent age of the social media, the concept of employer branding is so much more important than ever before.

We live in a transparent world. Curious about that restaurant on the corner? Google it and a bunch of Yelp or TripAdvisor reviews come up. If you don't trust those sites, you put the word out to your friends and their friends and inevitably someone has eaten there and can share their perspective.

The same things happen with companies and their reputations among job seekers. There are equivalent sites to Yelp, like Glassdoor.com, in which employees review their experience working at companies.

But just as importantly, word of mouth spreads. It spreads about what it's like to work for you, it spreads about the news of your company, and it spreads about how your company treats job seekers.

Focus on the Seeker

Remember, your startup has little to no brand in the mind of the job seeker. There are only a few ways that they would end up on your company's website. If you're lucky, it's because they use your product and it impressed them enough to check you out further.

First, you need to take off your product manager or engineer hat and put on your marketing hat. Employer branding is about *marketing your company to job seekers.*

More likely, they reached your site through someone they knew or through a cold job ad. You are trying to tell a story to the seeker. Chapter 1 of that story is the job ad itself.

Your 'About Us' page and your 'Leadership' page should be written, at least in part, for job seekers. This is a tough one, because you will also be writing these for prospective customers, partners, and investors.

Pro Tip 1: Have a 'Work for Us' or 'Careers' page on your website that is *specifically* for job seekers. You can customize the content here, so it can be a little different from the 'About Us' section of your site. Explain who you are, what you do (in plain English) and why it's exciting. This is a place to sell.

Pro Tip 2: Have an active job seeker read your 'About Us', 'Leadership', and 'Work for Us' pages of your website to see if they effectively convey the story of your company.

How Do I Build an Employer Brand?

An employer brand for a startup is something that can be, and probably should be, built sequentially over time. Because your company doesn't have much history, you won't have much, if any, visibility in the market with job seekers.

A few questions to answer as you start building:

1. *How do I best communicate the mission of the business?*

Job seekers need to feel the founding team's excitement for solving the customer's problem and the potential to disrupt an industry. You can be excited without being salesy.

If the business has traction in the form of customers, funding, partnerships, revenue or development, try to communicate that to seekers so that they can feel the momentum.

All people want to be successful, and be associated with successful companies and successful people. Tie into that desire by making seekers feel like your startup will be successful.

2. *What do I expect the career path will be for this employee and most employees? What kind of growth opportunities will I offer them?*

If you have a history in current or previous companies of internal promotions, this is a good place to describe it. See if you can highlight some examples.

3. *Do the founders, board members, advisors, or early hires have impressive track records?*

Especially if your startup is at a really early stage, showcase the background of the founders and why people would bet on them to win in this market. Use your advisors or angel investors (or anyone) to convey a positive impression.

A few simple things I advise against:

1. Don't only put pictures with links to LinkedIn profiles and Twitter profiles without any text description or bio. It's easy, but it's also lazy and it

doesn't serve your job seeker. If they are checking out the 'About Us' page and the founders, they want to know more. It's your job to curate and communicate. Don't make the seeker click and scroll through your LinkedIn profile.

2. Don't list every employee alphabetically. Seekers want to understand the leadership of the business and your background. Having all the employees is fine in a small company, but put them after the founders and leaders.

The 'Work for Us' or "Careers" Page of Your Website

Every company is different in terms of mission, stage, origin story, and so on; there is no perfect, universal advice here.

The most important thing to do is to take a good hard look at how you are describing the company *in the eyes of a prospective employee* who does not know you. Rewrite one or two paragraphs to change the customer or press perspective over to the employee perspective. Keep it clear of lingo and insider acronyms.

Next, gather feedback from someone who doesn't know the company; have them read and critique it.

Also, think hard about where you want this part of your website to go. Neil Costa, President of recruitment advertising agency Hireclix (whose interview is next) suggests having "Careers" be its own section of your website, not underneath the "Company" section but stand-alone. This will increase visibility, and therefore traffic, to these pages and to your jobs.

Job Descriptions

Job descriptions are a very important part of an overall employer brand. Startups often make some common mistakes, reminiscent of big companies' hiring practices.

Whether job seekers learn about your company from their network or a cold job ad, they will eventually get to a job description (also called a position description). Make your job descriptions interesting and exciting. Describe what the person will actually do without a lot of filler, such as internal company acronyms or jargon.

A job description is a stand-alone document, so don't assume that the seeker read all the interesting bits of your website or watched your videos there. In many cases, if the job description is poor, the seekers won't reach your website.

Sometimes startups try too hard to sound cool and relevant, filling their descriptions with industry buzzwords as well as words like "ninja" or "rock star". These are bound to get an eye roll from most candidates.

You don't need any of that. You just need to tell the applicant what they will do, why it's interesting and important, and a bit about your company's mission. You probably want to include a bit about who is a good fit in terms of values and tasks they like to do.

There are some examples of what I consider to be good "Careers" pages and good job descriptions in the bonuses for this book, which you can read at
www.entrepreneurrocketfuel.com/bonus.

How Do I Promote an Employer Brand?

Just like in all marketing campaigns, you want to try to be where the consumers are. In this case, consumers are jobseekers, so your promotion needs to be on the major job sites like Indeed.com

But also, emphasize social media and other research sites that seekers use like Facebook, Twitter, Glassdoor.com and perhaps Instagram.

Lastly, use word of mouth liberally. Tell people that you are hiring. Ask old friends and colleagues.

Who Drives the Employer Branding

For senior executives in a startup, particularly CEOs, it would be a huge mistake to think of employer branding as an HR activity. After all, recruiting is HR and HR should handle this, right? Wrong!

First and foremost, new employees join startups because of the reputation of the CEO and other founders, and the mission of the company. They are joining you on your journey into the unknown.

A Harvard Business Review study showed that 60% of CEOs believe the primary responsibility for employer branding lay with the CEO[3]. With startups, this is almost universally true given the importance of the founder's origin story and founding mission to job seekers.

While other executives and HR can help execute the campaigns, the definition of an employer brand must be driven by founders. Along with professional marketers, founders will best define the excitement of the company's vision. Even more, they can communicate the reasons why new employees want to come work there.

Don't get me wrong—I am not saying that HR shouldn't play a role. HR should make sure that the brand is effective

---

[3] Harvard Business Review, May, 2015, https://hbr.org/2015/05/ceos-need-to-pay-attention-to-employer-branding

and, most importantly, that it doesn't run afoul of any regulations. Companies can send subtle and not-so-subtle messages to candidates, some of which are sexist, ageist, or otherwise discriminatory. HR will also have a sense of what candidates are looking for, especially if those HR folks come from a recruiting background rather than a generalist or benefits background.

Regardless of who drives the definition of the brand, it is important that the *whole company* is part of promoting and executing it. Everyone needs to feel ownership here. They have a huge vested stake in who their future colleagues are going to be.

Hiring Process: Part of the Employer Brand

People often don't consider one other element that is a critical part of your employer brand: your hiring process.

It is a really easy thing to overlook. Founders often think, "We're a startup; we know how to hire and we don't want a lot of process."

It's true that you don't want to have an overly cumbersome process, laden with approval layers and HR-speak. Anyone who has ever applied for a job at a big company knows what I am talking about—the long and confusing online form, the multiple callbacks, the changing budget, multiple interviews where people ask you the same questions, etc.

But even startups need some process.

Ultimately, your hiring process will be the taste you leave with the job seeker as they interact with your company. Why spend time, energy, and money getting job seekers in the door if you aren't going to treat them well? Just like with other forms of bad "customer service," the word will get out.

That company? You don't want to apply there. They brought me in for an interview and never got back to me.

Or

They brought me in but couldn't make up their mind and brought me back three times before finally saying no. What a pain in the ass!

Word of mouth is powerful and spreads fast, especially in the startup community.

Build Only What You Need

Try to match the effort and complexity of your employer branding, and your recruiting process, to the stage of your company. When your product is in alpha, you don't spend a ton of money on a complicated website.

Similarly, your employer branding efforts should not be overly complicated or expensive when you are an early stage company. For example, when two founders are looking to hire one more person, you don't need much process at all. Most likely, you'll find your next employee or two from your own network or from word of mouth.

When you're trying to hire five to ten people in the seed stage, you will start to implement employer branding efforts. You don't need every bell and whistle at this point. You need the basics. You need to define what you represent to employees and a basic "work for us" website with a video.

As your growth rate increases and you start hiring in larger numbers, you need to up your game. In the same way that your marketing grows more sophisticated, more professional, and has broader reach, your employer branding efforts also improve and increase their reach.

Interview with Neil Costa, Founder & CEO, Hireclix

Hireclix is a recruitment advertising agency that helps employers manage recruitment advertising and build their hiring brand. Before founding HireClix, Neil was an executive at MyPerfectGig and Monster.com.

Rob Kornblum:
So how important do you think it is for a startup to build a hiring brand? And how can a startup with very little resource try to do that?

Neil Costa:
I think that it is critical for a company of any size to have some sort of brand and identity. So many companies are hiring, that as a recruitment marketing agency, we're trying to look for a unique story to tell.

Not everybody has a story to tell that people can connect with. They [might] have free snacks and foosball. Sometimes we're just trying to figure out how do we help them to [present] their story, which does generally come from the top. How does the leader engage with their employees, and get candidates to join the team?

So many times, startups are all geographically concentrated, and typically looking for engineers and salespeople. So all of these startups are looking for the same functional roles, in the same location, so what are you going to do that's going to make you stand out?

I think they have to have a unique story that people can connect with.

Right. [Some founders are] used to either hiring directly or working with recruiters, so maybe take a couple minutes and talk about what a recruitment advertising agency is and does. Then we can talk about how you guys work with clients to build those stories.

The mission of recruitment advertising agencies is to help you figure out where to advertise to find talent. That's our overall mission—how do we find the vehicles and help you tell the story to drive actual candidates and drive your employer brand?

And you help people build those stories?

We help them develop the creativity that [communicates] those stories, and then we help find the advertising vehicles to get the stories out there. It started off as very much digital—job postings, pay-per-click, things like that. As we've evolved and become more of a full-service agency, we're doing billboards, bowling alley ads, movie ads, in-theater 30-second spots, we've done radio now. So out of a digital marketing background, we had to continue to evolve to tell the story of our clients.

And so an employer brand is similar to a B2B or consumer brand, in that it tells a story. How is [an employer brand] different from those?

I think [an employer brand] should be answering the question, "why should I work here?" How am I going to be valued, how am I going to be successful?" When we were first starting... we saw some very distinct examples where traditional ad agencies would actually splinter off from the regular brand. And almost too far, to create this battle between corporate marketing and HR and things like that. So we tend to try and get people [on the same page].

Got it. And so it has a piece of the overall corporate mission, but it takes that and turns it.

And how have you seen the most successful startups communicate that? Both in the storytelling and some of the tactical elements.

I think [storytelling is] hard for a lot of companies... When we talk about stories, we're looking for authenticity. How does someone tell a unique story that is believable? That feels like it's coming from the heart, like it's a genuine person telling the story about their experience.

On the tactical side of things, you see people make decisions— the simplistic example is stock photo versus [photos of] actual employees. And this is controversial: "If I use actual employees, I have to get their release and if they leave do I still want to use them in my materials?" It could turn into this tactical nightmare. But if you use stock photos, can you find some stock photo that looks authentic and feels real?

And isn't just three smiling people around the laptop.

Right! So authenticity is really important, and it's hard to do that as a company gets bigger. For example, when you look at Marc Benioff [of Salesforce], you've got this great story where he's really committed and involved. His DNA is all over the culture there. Other companies just use all stock photos of some giant corporate entity that just comes across as disingenuous.

Let's cover some of the tools that a startup has available. So there's an "About Us" section of every website, but it's usually written for customers...So, tactically, do you suggest that there's a different description that gets written for prospective employees?

Yeah, we generally recommend that "Careers" [section of the website] be at the top-level navigation, preferably at the top of the page rather than buried at the bottom near the footer. If [hiring is] important to you, it really warrants a direct off-ramp to get to that page. When you get to Careers underneath About Us, you're just kind of burying it. It's just fundamental digital marketing; adding clicks will kill your conversion rate.

That's a really interesting point. Within that Careers page, what are some of the really important elements [where] you find your most successful clients operating?

I think that there's got to be an easy way to navigate to the jobs. When you've actually invested money in ads to get someone to the career site, let's make it as easy as possible for them to search for the jobs.

[We] don't want it to just be a directory listing, but it should be easy to find. If you looked at 100 websites, you'd find that half the time, you're struggling to figure out how to actually search for the jobs in a clean way.

In addition, we want to keep the copy succinct. We're dealing with a consumer environment that's got a very short attention span. Certainly as you move to the younger demographic, people are used to consuming content in very small bites. So, whether it's the Career pages themselves or the job descriptions, the text-heavy 3,000-word job description with 75 bullet points, it's just not going to work. And one of the worst things, on each job description, sometimes companies will put their company intro at the top of the job description on every single job description.

So we talk about advertising, and what placement is above the fold and below the fold. A company intro to greet you on every single job description is the most boring content above the fold in every scenario. There's a couple things between keeping the copy succinct and with some personality; some of that authentic personality of the company that you come across would be great. And we think video content is already being packaged in those—

Certainly, the explosion of video in every other format would tell you it's probably important in recruitment as well.

It is, [and you] don't have to go high production, I think we just need something that's consistent with the brand and easily digestible. [You're] trying to find a human to relate to and say, "I'm going to go through the trouble of applying for this job." Sometimes it's cumbersome, given some applicant tracking systems could be three minutes or 30 minutes, to get through and have your resumé ready and upload this and upload that. So we've seen a lot more clients go to more of a lead capture model.

So let's capture the lead, whether it's a hiring manager or a recruiter [who] will then go check out that person on LinkedIn and then you can do more of a progressive profile building to get the final application.

So just from a conversion perspective, we'd rather get leads and have the recruiting team work those leads. Or have us use a CRM to send out segmented emails to address those folks. That's a big change in recruiting in the last few years.

That makes sense. It's sometimes as if HR teams don't ever put themselves into the position of an applicant. And so [the application process] is really cumbersome.

Yeah, and I think sometimes there's a little bit of a Frankenstein application. You started off with maybe 10 questions and then over time, for compliance reasons, you needed to add [additional] questions, [then more] questions for something else, and you have a couple screening questions. Really, I think that [the] candidate experience is something that is still not treated in the same way as if you were selling product. Generally, recruiting is several years behind consumer marketing.

What are some best practices in candidate experience, that startups can adopt and be nimbler than some of these bigger companies?

I think that a lot of times startups under 100 people are missing opportunities by using a webpage with an email address, going into some hr@companyX. [Probably] that's the easiest thing to set up, but I think you're not creating any type of experience for them to leave a lasting impression or the chance to find those people they might relate to.

I think companies really want to create a little more structure than a cover letter and email from an email address. There are relatively inexpensive applicant tracking systems that have lead capture, with more matching through formal applications than just email and spreadsheets, that allow you to do some qualifying questions.

And that missed opportunity mostly comes from the ability to manage leads, you think? And build that longer-term relationship with candidates?

[If you have] a bunch of people that are going to go into an individual's mailbox folder, [then there is] no way to [continue to communicate] with the entire audience of interested candidates. Even having three or four questions like, "Have you worked at a startup before?" You could maybe start with those people [who have startup experience]. Three to five questions would be an ideal opportunity for some sort of light assessment on whether they are fit for your company.

I think that building up that video content, and things like that, is the stage of most startup companies; you're best doing it with your iPhone and as efficiently as possible to deliver that authenticity. But when you have a budget and just the email, you forgo the ability to track it really. You don't have any source codes or anything like that. Even for our own hiring needs, we'll usually put some money on every job that we have and start it up there, on Indeed.

And do you see that to be true for engineers as well?

I think that it's really challenging to try and find engineers on LinkedIn. We feel like the market's a little bit burnt out. But we still do really well in looking for engineers on Indeed. I think part of it is the clean interface. Part of it is the efficiency of the alert [functionality].

Indeed now offers this thing called Indeed Prime, [where] they're trying to practically qualify engineers and say, "Are you interested in a new job in the next 60 days?" They'll... do a technical assessment; they get a score and then they basically act as a job concierge for them. I think Indeed's doing some things to actually cater to a full-service candidate side. It's certainly a little bit more hand-holding and qualification to prep [the candidate] if they're ready to make a move.

What are some other best practices you've seen over your last six, seven, eight years, in working with startups who have really exploded their hiring? Somebody who's gone from 10 employees to 100. And the things that you've seen them do in building that brand and conveying it most effectively.

One of the things that's really impactful for early stage companies is hiring events: job fairs, career fairs, open houses. They feel a little bit old-school, but when done correctly, you're able to do a lot of things with hiring events. We really encourage them, especially at that early stage because, typically, you've got some positive news and momentum in the marketplace; you have a little bit of brand recognition because of funding or a new client or whatever it might be.

When you invite people [into] that startup environment, it's a little more casual so it almost feels more like a networking event. And then we typically are able to track [them;] we actually try and get people to pre-register, rather than rolling the dice at an open house in the old days. Just given the way we track campaigns, we can actually figure out if we have 150 people registered. We have some sense of who's going to come, some assurance for the executive team that this is going to be a worthwhile event or it's going to be a total dog.

And then once they get to the event, it's two things. With pre-registration, we see how many people are coming. But we can actually have the recruiters or hiring managers go through and look at their LinkedIn profile and cherry-pick them. Like, "Hey, I saw you registered for the event. Maybe we can set up a one-on-one with you and Rob while you're here." And so there's this high touch, authentic, concierge-type feel to coming in to the event, but we're going to pull you over and have a conversation with the VP of Engineering while you're here.

If you have a founder speak or you have somebody who's a technology thought-leader speak, you're showing a little bit of what [it's like to work there]. Almost like you'd get out of an all-hands meeting in a small company.

So that's probably one of the best ways. And still relatively cost-effective.

And you're right, it is counterintuitive in a digital world. Do you find those are effective even with a millennial population?

Absolutely. I think everybody wants to kick the tires, get in the office. Most the time we'll try to have the client do it in the office, but if it's a bigger company, we might have it at a venue. For this kind of startup, having their own single company hiring event is a really unique thing to consider at this stage.

Right, so it's an open house. How do you drive traffic to that? In the same way, using digital means in the same way you'd drive traffic to a posting?

Absolutely, yes. So we use all the similar channels, Google, Facebook, Craigslist...Indeed has an event-based posting we used. So it's really just a matter of putting it out there, having the employees share it. "Hey, I've got an employee sharing a bunch of job postings. Hey, we're having a hiring event."

When you generally have job postings, there's not always a really hard end date to your campaigns. However, when you have a hiring event, there's an end date we're all working toward.

Interesting. And how often would you suggest a startup have something like that?

I think once a quarter is a good idea...[generally] after hours. I think [lunch time is] an option as well.

I hadn't really thought of that as a tool that I think a lot of startups would use effectively.

We're trying to humanize the company and give it personality and give them somebody to connect with. And I think that makes a big difference in the recruiting process.

That is fantastic. Thank you.

Developing A Hiring System

Why Do You Need a System?

With so much to do, the vast majority of startup CEOs work on a "just-in-time" basis, meaning that they focus on the current priority of the day.

Hiring is such a big part of the founders' jobs, though, that they should move out of just-in-time mode, focus on the moment, to a much more strategic model of sourcing candidates.

Think about a startup CEO's job description. Fred Wilson, legendary venture capitalist, once described a startup CEO's job:

> *"A CEO does only three things. Sets the overall vision and strategy of the company and communicates it to all stakeholders. Recruits, hires, and retains the very best talent for the company. Makes sure there is always enough cash in the bank."*

So if you have a system for product management and getting out products, and a system for monitoring your cash balance, then you need a system for recruiting and hiring. I would go one step further, though. Not only do you need a system for hiring in the moment, but you need a system to stay a few steps ahead of the hiring needs of the company. You need a system that ensures you spend a significant portion of your time on hiring and people management.

Hiring, people management, and culture are that important!

What Do We Mean by a "System"?

I would say that a hiring system is a combination of your strategy and tactics for filling open needs inside the company, for building a pipeline of talent, for backfilling departures or firings, and for assessing possible executive level upgrades. There are two components to a company's hiring system.

1. The process by which you locate, interview, assess, reference check, offer, and onboard talent inside the company. Part of that should be the definition of the role and the success criteria for that position.

2. An equally important, and often missing part of a CEO's (or senior executive's) hiring system, is their model for building and keeping pipeline.

It happens all the time that an urgent hire needs to be made in a particular function. Why is it so urgent?

- The person you just put in did not work out and there wasn't a fit.
- The person you thought was great left for another role in a different company. Maybe they got offered more money, or a shorter commute, or something.
- The company grew and the needs of the role changed, or the VP didn't scale to the new requirements.

The reasons are varied, but incredibly common, so pipeline building is one of the most important parts of your job as CEO.

Defining the Role

Depending on the stage of your startup, defining the role of a new employee can either be rather easy or really challenging.

In an early-stage business, change and variability is a constant, so you want to keep the role definition somewhat open. For example, when hiring a junior marketing person, you might think she is going to focus on content creation and lead generation.

A month or two after they are hired, you decide that your business is going after larger accounts and switch the marketing to targeted "account-based marketing" which changes her role significantly. This happens all the time in startups.

Because of this variability, I have seen some startup clients of mine choose to stay very loose when defining roles (and objectives for those roles). I think this is a mistake. If you don't define the role, or the success criteria, then you have no idea what you are hiring for, other than likeability and resilience.

Defining the role helps you hire and it also helps your new employee hit the ground running. If the definition changes subtlety, people will adapt. If it changes radically, then you and the employee can jointly assess if the employee is a good fit for the new role.

Pipeline Building

What would you do if one of your most important team members quit?

Maybe she left and took another job, or his ailing mother has cancer. It doesn't really matter why. What are you going to do about it?

Your new VP of Engineering, the one you knew was going to do a great job is feuding with your co-founder and CTO, the product team doesn't like him; you have to let him go.

Or yet another hypothetical. Your company has grown, and your marketing head just isn't up to the challenge of managing a larger team and a larger budget. He was really hands-on two years ago, and you needed that back then, but now you need a more strategic person. You will need to upgrade.

The solution to all of these challenges is to keep an active pipeline of talent in a number of different functions at multiple levels.

Let's start with one function to show you how it is done.

- Through your own professional network, your board, and your other investors, make a list of all the great marketing people you know.
- Reach out to them and have a conversation or a meeting to explain your startup.
- Explain that you are not looking right now but that you always want to meet great people.
- Ask them for other people they know, up and comers, "A players" with various marketing skills. The most important areas to focus on are your direct reports and your most significant key contributors.
- Keep notes from your conversations and begin building a list using any method you find easiest: a database, an Excel sheet, note cards, whatever. Follow up, both with the people you meet and with the A players they suggest that you should know.

Again, it is critically important that you express that YOU ARE NOT HIRING NOW but that you are always looking to meet great people. This is for two reasons. First, you don't want to lead on anyone and let them think that you are networking because you have a job opening. The second key reason is that you don't want the word to get back to your current employees that you are out looking. You will spook them for no reason and give them reason to wonder if their job is safe.

This type of method, meeting A players and asking for referrals to other A players, is the best way to build and maintain a regular pipeline of talent. It IS a lot of work. But it is totally worth it. Keeping the company filled with A players is one of your most important jobs as a leader of a high-growth company. You will need to carve out a large portion of your calendar for hiring activities, including pipeline building.

Time Allocation

Between pipeline and regular interviewing, hiring should regularly take 20% to 40% of a CEO and founder's time. If it isn't, you may need to step up your activity if you want to scale.

Most of the time, when I talk to CEOs who are struggling hiring, they usually aren't getting enough people in the door, and they certainly aren't getting enough of the *best* people. Usually, this is a top-of-the-funnel problem. Just like with a marketing/sales funnel, if you don't generate leads and fill the top of the funnel, you won't generate closes.

In hiring, you have to spend a large portion of your time in outbound communication. Part of the reason it has to be you, and not a recruiter, is that people like getting messages from someone they may work for, but they don't like getting recruiter messages. You can have other people on the team help with outreach.

Interviewing

This is one of the most important aspects of bringing on "A players". It takes time to learn how to interview well (there is no single 'one way'), but doing so can maximize the chance that you will make good hires.

The stakes really go up when hiring in a startup. You want to ensure that there is alignment about expectations, and ensuring the candidate's fit for your values is critical.

If you are new to interviewing, I suggest trying to outline a set of "guiding principles." Jeff Bezos, the founder of Amazon, outlined his guiding principles for interviewing, which he directs his managers to use:

1. Will you admire this person [the candidate]?
2. Will this person raise the level of effectiveness of the group they are entering?
3. Along what dimension might this person be a superstar?

These have stood up as Amazon has grown to over 500,000 employees.

The founders that I have spoken with for this book, and elsewhere, emphasize two things: behavioral interviewing and something I am calling "real-world evaluation" or "experiential interviewing."

Behavioral interviewing moves away from standard interview questions like "tell me about yourself" to discover how the candidate acted in specific previous employment situations. Behavioral interview questions often start with "Talk about a time when..." and describe a situation they are likely to encounter in the role.

One challenge for behavioral interviewing is if the candidate has not worked in a startup before. This should not rule them out, but you will want to find other, non-work, situations which might reveal their adaptability, resiliency, or comfort with learning very quickly.

Most of the founders interviewed for this book utilize behavioral interviewing techniques. A few of them, like Sean Byrnes and Mark Godley, take this further to a real-world evaluation. Byrnes said:

"Our interview process [at Outlier] is really just a job simulation. We give you a problem that is very typical for the job that you'll have, and you work on it. You send us in a written solution. For developers that might be design or code. For a customer success manager, it may be an engagement or deployment plan. For product manager, it might be a product roll-out plan. And then when you come in to visit us, the day becomes essentially a simulation as if you were an employee with that job at the company, talking about the work that you proposed, and poking holes in it, and challenging it, and talking about it.

[You're] testing 'How they would do in the job if they had it?' Usually everybody walks away with a very strong sense of whether or not they would do a good job, and whether or not they want to do the job.

I find that that is the only process I have found that is predictive of success. Every other interview process that I've ever seen has almost no correlation, if not negative correlation, with eventual success in a job."

Marco Rogers has interviewed over 400 candidates as an engineering lead at Yammer, Lever, and Clover Health.[4] One of the most important things he discovered was that you really don't know what you need. You are figuring it out as you go. For example, with engineers, leaders often try to hire for a specific language or mostly for technical skills, and this assumption often turns out to be incorrect.

A few other tips that Rogers suggests:

- Reduce Bias: Multiple people in an interview can help reduce bias, and it helps to separate the act of

---

[4] Published interview- http://firstround.com/review/my-lessons-from-interviewing-400-engineers-over-three-startups/

asking a follow up question from listening deeply to the candidate.

- Integrated Interview: Have everyone on the team interview. It takes a lot of time, but it is a critical business skill.

- Interview *More* Candidates: Rogers believes that initial filters and screens are often very flawed. Broadening the funnel smartly will bring in people whose LinkedIn profiles may not reveal that they kick ass.

- Huddle: Getting your team together quickly to discuss candidates will reveal much more than written notes, and will show you a lot about your team as well and what they value.

To see a list of interview questions, and to learn more about behavioral interviewing techniques for startups, check out the free bonuses for this book at: *www.entrepreneurrocketfuel.com/bonus*

Reference Checking

Checking references is a critical step in hiring in any company, but especially in a startup where your mistakes are amplified. Do not skip the references and do not speed through this part of the process. Also, don't let HR or a recruiting firm do reference checks. Hiring managers need to do this and get good at it.

First, it is important to check references broadly. Do not just accept the list of references that the candidate provides. Try to speak with past bosses, peers and perhaps customers or partners. Use LinkedIn to see if you know people who they worked for or worked with.

One way to get a broader list it to simply ask for more from the provided references. "Is there anyone else I can speak with about "Bob," someone who would have a good perspective?"

Second, use the same list of questions for all of the references. That makes it easy to consolidate information and look for patterns.

The book _Who: The A Method for Hiring_ by Geoff Smart and Randy Street suggests the following questions (and this is certainly a good starting place):

1. In what context did you work with the person?

2. What were the person's biggest strengths?

3. What were the person's biggest areas for improvement back then?

4. How would you rate their overall performance on a 1-10 scale? What causes you to give that rating?

5. The person mentioned that they struggled with _____ in that job? Can you tell me more about that?

Third, listen for "coded" responses in reference checks. People rarely want to tell the truth about someone if it's negative. It is important to read between the lines. Significant hesitation or "faint praise" can be warning signs.

Don't be scared off by one or two negative references—not everyone is going to do well in all situations with all people. If you get some negatives, that is probably a sign to probe deeper.

Hopefully this chapter and the interviews in the book have given you ideas about how to develop your own "system" for hiring into your "rocket ship" startup.

Interview with Steve Hafner, Founder & CEO, Kayak

Steve Hafner is the Founder and CEO of Kayak, the online and mobile travel site used by hundreds of millions of consumers. Hafner founded Kayak in 2004, guiding it to a public offering and ultimately an acquisition by Priceline for $1.8 Billion.

Rob Kornblum:
Steve, it's my understanding when you started Kayak and decided to work with Paul English that you guys hadn't worked together before?

Steve Hafner:
Absolutely true. We met a couple days before deciding to found Kayak.

Given the importance of that decision, working with a co-founder, how did you know that you could work well with Paul or that he could work well with you?

Well, we didn't. It was a leap of faith for both of us. Basically, I sat down and pitched him the idea of Kayak with the intention of accessing his network to find people who could build it because I couldn't write a line of code. Through the course of the lunch meeting he got excited about the idea, and then we just had this immediate rapport. We had both worked with a lot of people in the past, so you kind of know over time how to judge human talent and work style. A couple hours into the lunch we decided to start the venture, with full knowledge that it might not work out.

Was it always a split office from the beginning with you in Connecticut and him in Boston?

It was. [It is] not something I'd recommend with other startups, though it's easier [today] when you've got video conferencing and Slack, but we made it work. Both sides have just got to overly communicate and travel. I was in Boston two days a week. He was down here [in Connecticut] one day a week. I stuck to the commercial knitting. He stuck to building the product, and that seemed to work.

What were some of the things that made it work? How often were you guys face-to-face?

It started with a clear division of responsibilities. Connecticut is not known for top-notch tech talent, so it was pretty clear the technology was going to be in Boston. Our CTO [Paul] built the product. In Connecticut [we had] a great group of senior executives who knew finance, and marketing, and other commercial functions.

OK. Were you the de facto product visionary, because [I know that] you are super passionate about the [Kayak] product? How did that work in terms of your interface with the tech talent in Boston?

I love the product because when you operate a website or an app, everybody sees it and has an opinion about it, like a restaurant. I certainly had an opinion about the product, and I had the travel experience, but I wouldn't call myself a product guru. Paul and the tech team in Boston really led the charge on that. I could suggest ways of building the product or changing the product that reflected my days from Orbitz, but it was a collaborative group effort to be sure.

It was [kind of] a trade-off between church and state. Paul served the role of church, which was he wanted to build the simplest, most user-friendly product ever. As "the state", I was into the commercial parts, what was good for the airlines and our business partners, how could we get ads onto the app, et cetera. Not only could we build a great product, but we also had to make money providing that service. I think that dynamic actually worked really well.

How did you find your first couple of hires who were not founders? Were they people you knew? As you started to network outside those people, how did you sell them on the opportunity? How did you differentiate?

Sure, so our first 14 hires were in place in a week, and 12 were techies who came with Paul from Intuit or other companies. Then two were folks that I had worked with in the past at Orbitz or BCG.

That's roughly the proportions of Kayak as its grown. We're an engineering and technology company, so about 70% of our heads are in that. The other 30% are in the overhead functions, but we started with people we knew because the initial set of hires are the most critical ones and you don't have the luxury of being wrong. If you staff with people you work well with who are great recruiters in their own right, then you have a much higher probability of success.

Given that you and Paul hadn't worked together, tell me about the discussions around values and culture, and how you guys decided to build your team? What things were you looking for as you expanded outside the people you knew?

About two months into the forming of the company, we commissioned an external agency called Wolff Olins to help us come up with the cultural values and how we were going to run the company, which is very atypical for a venture-backed startup, right? We knew we had to get the foundation and the framework right from the get-go if we wanted to build a global organization. That's very different from how most companies start.

Part of what we were trying to do is to say what are the communication ground rules, particularly since we weren't working in the same locations. What are we looking for in people? What's our culture going to be like? We came up with a handful of stuff that I think served us well like being totally transparent, not having an agenda, having standup meetings, no big presentations, succeeding or failing fast. A lot of buzzwords now that a lot of companies adopt, but at the time was fairly radical.

Right, and an agency helped you walk through that?

Yeah. Paul and I went down to New York with a handful of our employees, sat in with the Wolff Olins folks, and just said, "Hey, what do you guys want to be when you grow up?" We just talked about the values that mattered to us in a two-day workshop.

We didn't like candy-coating. We like people who were direct and transparent and didn't have hidden agendas. We wanted healthy debate, but once we came to the decision, we wanted everyone to unite behind it.

Then how did you take that forward into the hiring process? How involved were you in those hires versus Paul, and how did you look to reinforce those things in your early hiring?

Well, it helped shape our candidate profiles and the interview questions, particularly around work style. Then we made sure that the candidates were interviewed across the different functional departments and offices, and that we each had veto rights. If someone has an assistant, we didn't hire them. You know, we still don't have assistants here.

[Another one was] "Do you know how to do a pivot table in Excel?" You'd be surprised how many financial folks don't know how to use a pivot table. Simple stuff; we wanted people who did their own work versus relying on a team to do it for them.

Right, and that was important to reinforce, even with your managers, this is place where people do—not just manage.

Paul [English] has been in the news a bit about how he went about the hiring system, which is really pretty differentiated. Kayak really seemed to use speed as a competitive advantage in the hiring process. I'm sure it was part of a broader kind of hiring and talent managing agenda?

One of the few advantages we had over existing companies was the speed at which we could execute: hiring, recruiting and training, implementing, getting product out there, and learning from user engagement. Paul and I took that philosophy into how we brought people onboard, and a lot of it was just trial by fire. If we saw someone that we really liked, we put out all the stops to get that person onto the team. I've realized over time the downside to that approach: it doesn't really scale well. We didn't have enough time to train or onboard our people properly. Which works great when there's 40 people, but not so great when you're 1,000 people like we are today.

Right. Tell me about scaling.

As a management team, we came to realize that there are people who can take you to a certain level; they individually don't scale beyond that.

You just need to make a decision, to hire a different profile above them, or below them, or replace them. That's the kind of decision making that I think every CEO or co-founder wrestles with over time.

At some point in time Kayak's going to outgrow me. It probably already has, but we just haven't found someone better to do it.

It's a super hard thing though as a founder. [You have got] super loyal people who got you to where you are...How do you reach that conclusion, and how do you have that difficult conversation?

Usually it's mutual, so the person knows they're out of their league, and you both want the entity to succeed. Given our culture of being transparent and direct we really never had an issue with anyone. Maybe we just got lucky that way, but since the company was successful, we had no problem placing those talented people at other companies. Our VCs loved approaching our own team for their other portfolio companies.

Okay, and so you certainly are a proponent for de-risking, working with people you've worked with before in terms of really understanding their work style and how they're going to operate in the trenches?

Yeah. For sure. The first thing we needed was someone who could fly around and get commercial agreements with the airlines and online travel agencies, so we would get paid. Then we needed a product, so we hired a bunch of people to build that product. Then the next two critical hires were marketing to get an audience to use the product, and then finance to actually make sure that we could count the money. Those were people I knew. I got our CMO, our general counsel, a bunch of people from Orbitz.

I want to go back to culture for a second, as you looked to build out the team and you grew through the 'messy middle', moving from product market fit, but before aggressive scaling (say 40 or 50 people)...I'm interested to hear where you fall on two schools of thought in terms of culture. One is, you've got to be really rigorous about hiring for culture because all those people have got to fit. On the other hand, certain CEOs are looking for culture adds; fit is a little bit of a codeword for bias...

Yeah. I would probably err towards the latter than the former. We were always looking to add voices and fresh eyes to our team to de-risk or limit the potential that we weren't seeing all the opportunities. We didn't try to hire the best people in the travel business. We tried to hire the best, super talented, people in any category. You didn't need domain expertise. So, when we took Kayak to Europe we wanted to make sure that we had someone who knew the European mindset on product, et cetera. That was nobody we knew at Kayak through our own networks.

If it was clear that it was not a fit, then we would find a soft landing and a quick exit for them. Particularly if they were bullies or idiosyncratic. Then for the people who were super talented, but might fit with some coaching, we tried to coach them for a little bit. That's not really our strength here, so ultimately a lot of those people exited too.

Right. How much time did you (and do you) spend hiring and on the internal team?

Paul [English] had a passion for that, and he was excellent at it, much better than I was. He's just one of these guys that is charismatic and magnetic, and a great judge of people. He would go to a meeting with me. Let's say we were visiting Google to talk to them, and he would come out of that meeting with, "Hey, we should go grab this person."

I'd be sitting in the meeting thinking about the topic matter being discussed, and he'd be thinking, "Hey, that person is really smart. We should steal them." He was always recruiting.

You mentioned the 'war for talent' when you were on stage at Dartmouth; how do you think about that now at scale? How do you make sure that you're still on top of it?

Ultimately, there's the plumbing, right? You need to have a great office environment, good compensation, and good teams that people like to work with, but really the higher ideal is to have an operating vision that motivates people, that they find inspiring.

That's the most important thing for us to get great talent. "Hey, we're doing something wonderful at Kayak. We're helping people experience the world. That's better than selling flavored soda water, or making printers, or computers." You need to have the higher vision, and all the other stuff is table steaks.

Right. For those companies that lose their way, like Yahoo, do you think they stumbled because they either didn't have or couldn't communicate that higher vision?

Yeah. That's a big part. The other part is they just had too many B and C players. A great vision attracts everybody. The second thing you need to do is you need to filter out the B's and C's. Yahoo had mis-stepped on that one very early on.

Right. At your scale, how do you avoid diluting the gene pool?

That's a good way to put it. You can just tell. If the person that you're interacting with is an A player, [you know]. A players just get frustrated with anyone that's not up to their [level]. They're always dissatisfied. They're always looking for a new way to do things, and if you're in a room with people who don't have those traits or characteristics you know it.

Now, what are your biggest organizational challenges? Not strategic, but really kind of within the context of your team.

You know, I always wanted to have a really small, highly motivated, impactful team. We're 1,000 people now, and we're going to be in 2,000 in a few months here because of an acquisition.

It's tough for me to have a personal interaction with all of those people, and to ensure that they're doing the right thing, first and foremost. Number two, that they're enjoying it. That means I have to trust the folks below me a lot more, which means I'm putting a much bigger load on each of my direct reports and the level right below them. Honestly, I can't interact with or coach more than 50 people on a regular basis to have their own trickle-down effect. That's really what I spend most of my time doing now.

How important is it for you to communicate the vision to the troops? Is it predominantly you to your direct reports, those 50? From them on down?

Yeah, so it's all of the above. Every opportunity we have to communicate the vision and our values, we do that. I send out monthly emails of how we're doing and stuff that we're working on.

I'm just curious how that's changed for you over the last few years. As you grew, you could stand on a chair and still speak to the whole room. Now, you either need a bigger room or a different way of communicating. How has that changed for you?

Yeah. In the early days you didn't have to talk about culture or vision because everybody would observe from what you were doing what was valued to you and what wasn't. Then you put pen on paper. You actually come up with a vision statement and you communicate that, but you still have to live it. You know, for us every opportunity we can.

We have what we call 'town meetings' in each of our offices once a month as well where we communicate that. Then two days a week, we have free meals and what we call 'open assemblies', where whoever is senior in the office, regardless of their office or department, takes Q&A from our employees. These are all opportunities to both communicate the vision as well as to take input from the folks who are actually doing the day-to-day work. To make sure that the two are aligned.

You feel good about those processes?

We're still working, but we're doing better these days than we used to.

Excellent. Alright, so I know you've stood on a couple of boards as you advise young companies. What's your number-one advice with regard to team-building and culture?

My number one advice is "don't underestimate how important team building is." A company is ultimately just a collection of people behind a shared vision. You want to make sure you have the right collection of people. You can insert any sports analogy you want, but it starts with the athletes and with a good coach. If you don't have the athletes, no great coach will be able to put it together. Ideally, you'll have both.

Hiring Early Executives

As you move past "survival mode" and figuring out your product, customer fit, and market, you will want to bring in team leaders ("executives") to run various functions.

In the previous interview, Steve Hafner of Kayak showed a desire to hire "[v]ery early on because, you know, if we didn't add executives we would have just stayed at a PowerPoint deck, which a lot of startups do. I hired our Chief Commercial Officer a week after we founded the company. We didn't hire a CMO or a CFO for a long time because those are really expensive positions, and we wanted the right people for that."

Buy-in from Your Team

When hiring your first executives, it is crucial to get buy-in from the other executives and founders. This is common sense, but we still see CEOs pursue hires with little or no approval from the existing team.

Other executives will bring a very different perspective from yours, the perspective of a peer. They will have to work side-by-side, in the trenches, with your new hire. There will be disagreements. You want them to be able to fall back on a shared respect, a sense of prior experiences and accomplishments.

Before the rest of your team meets a candidate, you should make sure that you have:

1) An open position;
2) A strong sense of who you are looking for, articulated in writing; and
3) A vision of success for the person filling the role.

Let's break these down.

Meeting with executives for networking purposes, or to build a hiring pipeline (a critical task, which I discuss in the previous chapter "Developing a Hiring System") is very different from meeting an executive for an interview because you have an open position which they might be able to fill. Make sure the objective is clear in your head, and that you make it clear to the executive when you first meet. I have witnessed networking meetings in which the CEO gets interested in the executive and asks him to meet with other members of the team right then and there. While I applaud the company's speed, it creates confusion for both the team and the executive, and is not likely to end well.

For an open position, write down the position description and the background of what you are looking for. Communicate the description and background to your team and get buy-in on the goals of the position before you start bringing in candidates. Your team can help you hone in on the best candidates, and possibly provide candidates' names.

Lastly, as part of our recommended hiring system, write down what success will look like for anyone filling the role. For example—within one year, you expect your new CMO to increase leads by 40%, increase significant media mentions through interviews and other publications, and refresh your website. When you and your team have a sense and vision of success, then you have a *much* better ability to hire for capability and cultural fit, and not just for likeability.

I recommend using a system, with minor adaptations, that I first learned in the book _Who: A Methodology for Hiring_, written by Geoff Smart and Randy Street. The authors recommend creating "score cards" for roles. Score cards for roles have three parts—a job's mission, it's outcomes (how you will define success), and competencies (basically a mix of skills and values).

Of these, I find the outcomes to be the most important tools that allow hiring managers to focus on the measure of success, and not on the day-to-day tasks.

You may also want to involve the people who will report to the executive. This can be a little tricky. Let's say you hired a director-level (one step below VP) marketing person who has been a critical part of building the business to your current state. You decide to hire a new CMO to get you to the next level. Your director-level employee might view it as a slight that they weren't offered the position.

However, there is another way to frame that situation for your director. First, it is rare that you get to help pick your new boss. Second, this new hire is a model for him/her and can help mentor him/her to get to the CMO position eventually. She gets to see how a CMO operates in a high-growth startup.

Be Careful of the Big Brands

One thing you want to watch out for is an executive whose experience is primarily or exclusively with large companies, even those in your space. Sure, if you're a software startup, it can be attractive to get someone who worked at Microsoft or Oracle or IBM.

The most significant downside to big company experience is that big company employees have LOTS of support around them and they may expect or need that support in your startup. It's hard to ask someone who is used to a big team to do a bunch of grunt work themselves, but that is what startups often require.

This can be particularly true in sales and in marketing at a startup, which is TOTALLY different from selling and marketing as a known brand. When you work for well-known companies like Microsoft or Salesforce, prospects take your call because they know your company. When you work for an unknown startup with no brand awareness, you need a different set of sales skills to pry open the door, and a different set of sales skills to convince the prospect to take a risk on your unknown company's solution.

That is a tough balancing act to find.

You don't want an exec who won't roll up their sleeves and get their fingers dirty; your early employees will resent their new boss if they appear too "above it."

On the other hand, you didn't hire a VP of marketing to personally pour through Google Analytics reports and craft the copy of every marketing email. You could hire an individual contributor for that, or a mid-level person. You hire a world-class executive for their expertise and leverage in building a great team under them.

So, what is the right balance between big company "successes" and startup challenges? Often, it is some combination of both. You want people still scrappy enough, but who bring some best practices and the big company Rolodex for sales and hiring purposes.

Balancing Senior & Junior Hires

A second huge challenge is to balance the seniority and expertise of the leadership team you want with the nimbleness and raw hunger of more junior people.

For example, you may not be able to afford or attract a Director or VP of Marketing in the early stage. Even if you can, the marketing job at that point is super hands-on, and requires a ton of resilience to try and fail multiple times. However, you want to attract a senior person for two reasons: they add credibility for investors and they are world-class in their field. They are *better than you* in marketing, which is what you want.

This is a difficult balance in terms of expense, execution, and fundraising. High-end senior executives are expensive, but you probably need them to fundraise effectively. You also want them so that you can spend less time in the functional details and more time on the strategy and overall business execution.

Hiring Executives Outside Your Functional Area

A third challenge, especially for first-time CEOs, is hiring an executive to lead a function in which the CEO has little or no expertise. For example, a product-oriented or technical founder who needs to hire a financial executive may have no idea if a VP of Finance or a CFO is needed, or the difference between them. Similarly, a sales-centric founder may struggle when they need to hire a CTO.

The Board of Directors can be helpful here, since they may be able to fill in the blanks in terms of the real requirements. They can also explain the difference between a CTO and a VP of Engineering, or the difference between a CFO and a VP of Finance.

However, some CEOs are reluctant to share their lack of knowledge in these types of matters with their Board members. They might feel it makes them look weak or inexperienced.

One of the best strategies, when you're faced with this situation, is to lean heavily on your network. Use the expertise of your advisors and your broader network to for guidance and getting familiar with what you don't know.

Have CTO friends help you prepare the job requirements. If you can, have them sit in on a couple of interviews. Lisa Skeete Tatum, founder of Landit (interviewed later in the book), did exactly that. She started the business and used outsourced development, but leaned heavily on her network to help interview and recruit her CTO.

Hiring an Executive in Your Functional Area

One of the trickiest roles to fill is for an executive who will lead a function in which you have the most experience; if you're experienced in product management, this would be your VP of Product. If you ran sales, this would be your VP of Sales.

The first common challenge is in the hiring process itself. CEOs with strong knowledge of a particular function bring some strong biases to "the way things should be done." After all, they did them a certain way and that way worked for them.

The second major challenge is in managing an executive who has been hired. Sometimes, the CEO will be far too hands-off, more so than in other functions. This leaves the new executive kind of "hanging" during the first year, without nearly enough guidance while integrating into the business.

The other more common issue is when the CEO tends to micromanage the executive in that function, even unintentionally; CEOs know so much about the function that they cannot help themselves. This frustrates the executives, who are used to having quite a bit of autonomy and have been successful in their own right.

Board Advice

Board advice on executive hiring is a lot like seasoning when you're cooking:

Not enough and you'll miss out.

Too much and you overdo it.

If you pay too much attention to executives in your Board's network, you may make bad hires. Executives who worked well in a prior portfolio company of your investor might not be perfect for your company. Your startup might be at a different stage, or might have a very different culture, than his/her last success.

On the flip side, it can be very tough to recruit top talent on your own, especially top talent with startup experience, who are well known and liked in the investor community. Avoiding leads from your investors and board would probably be a mistake.

By all means, take a look at candidates known by your investors, who will vouch for them. But also make sure you know what you need for your stage of growth, and which cultural elements are must haves, and have nots, for you.

Overall, hiring a team of executives who report to you represents an inflection point for your startup business. You have moved from the phase of survival, where everyone is doing whatever they need to do, to expansion and growth. You need team leads who can be trusted, who can lead, and who know more than you do about their particular function.

These people can be hard to find, hard to attract, and hard to compensate properly. I recommend leaving yourself a lot of lead time for these types of hires, and to be building your pipeline continuously.

Interview with Lisa Skeete Tatum, Founder & CEO, Landit

Lisa Skeete Tatum is founder and CEO of Landit, Inc., a startup seeking to help unlock workplace talent for employers and employees. She was previously a venture capitalist at Cardinal Partners.

Rob Kornblum:
So tell me more about Landit and what you guys are doing.

Lisa Skeete Tatum:
Absolutely. Our platform is geared to increase the success and engagement of women and others in the workplace. [There are] millions of women just trying to figure out how to more successfully navigate, or maybe they're somewhere feeling stuck and don't know how to get out of it. [As] you progress in your career, and the more challenging it becomes, the large number of professional, educated women not firing on all cylinders who want to be. And it's not for lack of skill, or track record, or motivation. It's not knowing where to start or not knowing what they don't know. And even if they did know, they don't have the access to what they need.

On the other side, companies realize that it's an economic imperative that they unlock the talent of everyone in the workplace. The problem is, they don't have a way to do that.

The company is no longer responsible for your career. You are. We have Fortune 500 companies that buy our technology to invest in their talent. And now anyone, regardless of level, regardless of gender, background, or schooling, now has equal shot at success.

People always talk about having a mentor. It's actually not about having a mentor. It's about who's occupying the five seats that we define: your mentor, your sponsor, your connector, your point expert, and then of course, everyone needs a close friend.

It is a highly personalized playbook. Almost like you're unlocking missions, if you will. So now we have the person who runs all of coaching at MIT, or some of the top coaches at Google, that previously were only available to a small slice of mortals, now can be available to anyone in the palm of their hands.

And then we have a piece on your personal brand. We know that personal brand accounts for 30% of what it takes to be successful. Most of us don't know it, don't even know the mistakes that we're making.

I want to transition to the team-building side of things. So your team is still pretty small?

Yes, we are. Small and mighty, punching well above our weight, for sure. Under 10 people.

Where did the first team members come from? Were they people you knew or people you found?

It [is] a balance. For quite some time, it was just me as I was trying to figure out what this thing was. But given that it is a tech company, finding a tech leader was job number one, two, three, and four. And finding not only someone who has the technical chops, but someone who not only got what we were doing, but where we were compatible. It took a very long time. I met a [ton of] candidates. So because I didn't know these folks, I utilized my advisors. I had tech giants, legends, angel investors that had founded multi-billion-dollar companies. I asked them, "Help me screen for fit and technical ability," etc. Did they understand the stage? Could they grow with what we were trying to do, etc.

So when I first started, I actually partnered with Pivotal Labs, which most seed-stage companies do not do because of the expense. So when I did find a technical partner, they would have a quality product from which to take and expand.

So I have been very, very judicious with who we bring on...Our first two hires were engineers; I didn't know either one of them, but they were extremely well vetted, and that worked out. The more recent folks I've pulled in have been people that I have known. And it's about pulling from your networks as well and making sure that people really understand what they're getting into. Because not everyone, as you know, is cut out for the startup world. And I've learned that in many different ways.

So how do you vet for that?

I screen for extreme curiosity and wanting to grow... Even at this stage in my career, I am a work in process. So just as the product innovating, I feel like I'm innovating and growing. And I need someone who gets the importance of disrupting themselves...I screen heavily for hustle factor because as we're on this mission, I and others will run through fires to figure it out. "Get knocked down, get back up"- that kind of hustle factor. I may not know the answers, but I'm going to figure it out.

But the other thing that's really important, just my own personal value, is I have a zero-drama rule...between trying to manage growing a company, my family, personal obligations, etc., any drama time [is] taking away from what we're doing to move the mission forward. So, intellectual curiosity, hustle factor, disrupt yourself, etc. But do not bring any drama to my doorstep.

[Just] personality-wise, the one time I bent on that, I regret it still to this day. Because you know, when you make a hiring mistake in a small company, each additional person you add either gives you tremendous leverage or tremendous strain. You cannot afford to make those kinds of mistakes. And if you do, and we all make them, you've got to take care of it right away.

How quickly did you know that it was wrong?

Not quickly enough.

Within 90 days for sure. Because you want to give people time [and room for mistakes]... But you have to look at intent [or] intention. And then you have to look at their ability to flex. When you are a seed-stage company, everybody can't just stay in their domain. So I'm the chief coffee pourer [and] the CEO and also I'm the founder. And I need others who want to flex. We all have expertise, but, when we look at something, we've got to move as a team...with the same mission and have the same work ethic. But I'm all about 1+1=10 when it comes to assembling a diverse team, diversity of thought, variance, etc.

I want to shift gears a little bit because you've been now a company builder and a VC. How did you think about building up and managing your board as a part of your team? And what have you done to really make that team successful?

Changing the world is hard. We talk a lot about...how to surround yourself in a way that's best in your favor. Like, who's putting the extra weight on your scale? And I very much believe in that saying that you are the average of the five people you spend the most time with. And so when I look at the board together, you're going to have your investors, but not all investors are the same, as you know. So who has expertise or connections, who'd be willing to help to work on our behalf. Right? We're not a high-maintenance group, but someone who would pick up the phone on your behalf, would make an introduction or be a thought partner.

But I also made sure that we had independence. [So] one of our strategic investors was one of my first board members because she had industry expertise...she was able to bring her lens of the landscape and what she has seen. Or Sheila Marcelo my co-founder, who also has a different [perspective]. So I looked at the yin to our yang almost. I was trying to figure out, who did I need? Who understood what we were trying to do [and] be honest with me?

But I work better when someone lays it out [honestly so I can move forward]. You know, "Lisa, would you consider this? Lisa, this is working." So I just look to kind of putting that together and keeping it small. But I have the official fiduciary board, then my [much broader] advisory board, and my personal board.

That makes sense. Some of those clearly are one-to-one relationships where you're both finding value in the connection. Are you trying to make them more a part of a cohesive group? Or what have you done [toward] that?

Yeah. I find that, particularly with these different circles, the advice generally happens one-to-one. But that's because lives and careers and spheres of influence overlap, that they also have linkages and connections. [Some of my board] actually already [knew] each other. But then I find them, not that Lisa convenes them and says, "Okay we're going to do xyz." But then because we're all together fostering those ties or that synergy piece.

What other things do you do for that, your employees? Is it behavioral interviewing? What things do you try to really drive that, to uncover how people are going to be in those tough times?

Actually, that's something new that we just started doing...It was recommended by a very successful private equity firm. we have our chart of Landit culture and what is important (what are we looking for), people are very clear what they're signing up for. But we also have this little assessment tool. Everyone on the team has taken it. It's on everything from pace to decision making, etc. So we know where we, as individuals, fall. And we have all said, for every single person on the team for that role, where do you think that person needs to be on all of these factors? So we use it as a tool. When someone takes it, you look at fit with the role, fit with the team...no, you can't rely 100% on just one tool. But it's been phenomenal for us. And I'll say [that] most people should do that.

Is it a tool you developed or one that was more on the shelf?

No, there's a [private equity] firm that does this for a living...they don't even interview you until you take this test. I am telling you, it is eye-opening. And as a leader, it will tell me [that] I'm falling off the charts in terms of moving fast. But if I have someone, and I do have someone on my team who's more deliberate, it then says, "When you're working with them, these are some things you want to consider." Or, I am very data-driven. So it tells my team, when you approach Lisa with something, you want to make sure ... she's going to ask you these types of things. And so it not only helps you screen, but since everybody does it, it actually helps with the transparency. of how we work more effectively together.

The other thing that we do, that we also borrowed from someone, is everyone [has] a user manual. And it literally is everything from what makes me tick to the one thing that people misunderstand about me, to what's the best time to communicate. And so when we're bringing someone on board, we deliver to them the user manual of every single person in the company.

That's really cool. Did you develop those?

Nope. It was recommended by another CEO and we just borrowed it. And it's great because it is everything from, again, the best time to communicate to what does it take to get me on board. I mean, everyone answers the exact same question but it's very, very enlightening; going back to my no-drama rule, you have to have transparency. Transparency of what's going on with the business. Transparency of how you work. Space for people to be open and honest, and bring their ideas and put it all on the table.

So that's the culture I'm trying to create and reinforce....We're putting everything on the line for what we're trying to do with Landit, and therefore, people got to line up behind that.

You had a long and successful venture career. When you were a VC, what were the things that you looked for or look for in terms of teams? What defined an A team versus not? And how did you use team as an element of thinking about the kinds of investments you would make?

We didn't always have an A team [to invest in], but I always wanted the A founder, someone who not only understood the pain point in the market, but was somehow uniquely positioned to execute. What I always look for is founder market product fit, or stacking the deck in your favor. Because if you have some product market fit, then even if it wasn't a full team, they would be able to assemble the team. I don't trust or believe anyone who says, "Yeah I've always wanted to be an entrepreneur." Because you have to be driven by something so much bigger than that because it's so damn hard. Right? It has got to be that you see something that you just can't stand it anymore...and are committed to solving that. And again, the only time we ever deviated from the A player, A team, we lost money. So that would be nice to have.

A lot of times, we were a seed [investor]. And when we were a [Series A investor], I would ask "who's that team? [How] do they work together?" I was always the one looking at dynamics in meetings. So if they were saying the right thing, but you could tell from some of those nonverbal cues, setting people off...I really cue into those things because someone will show you, not just tell you, who they are.

Got it. Did you look at or think about their ability to continue to build out from an execution perspective?

Oh, absolutely. If you have that fit, then they will be able to attract folks. And even if not, their expertise, they will attract people who do have that expertise. So you'd better believe it, because if you're building for scale, which... that's our job as investors...you have to have people who are going to be able to do that and do that wisely. And if you have a mediocre leader, they're going to hire mediocre people because they will hire [at their level] as opposed to hiring up. So, absolutely.

For a copy of a blank "User Manual" that Lisa uses, as well as the other bonuses associated with this book, go to www.entrepreneurrocketfuel.com/bonus

Onboarding

Here is an example of how having little to no onboarding will hurt your startup.

Charlie just accepted a position with a great new startup. After a little back and forth with the hiring manager, he signs the offer letter and determines a start date.

Charlie shows up at the office at 9:00 a.m. on the appointed date, but there really aren't a lot of people around yet. The guy who *is* there isn't sure who Charlie is or where he's supposed to sit. Charlie feels pretty uncomfortable, makes a little small talk, but inside he's wondering *"why doesn't anyone know I'm starting today?"*

As people start to arrive, someone knows where Charlie should sit, and leads him there. The table still has some coffee stains from the previous occupant, and what appears to be a remnant of leftover food. Charlie decides to be proactive, finds the kitchen and a sponge, and cleans off his area. But without a laptop or any instructions, he has to hang out for a while longer.

Charlie's manager is traveling to see a customer and isn't there to meet him that day. The interviewing team is glad to see him back, and shake his hand, but they didn't know he was starting and no one has a laptop for him. Someone remembers a spare and gets it, but Charlie doesn't have credentials to get into the email system, Slack, or any of the other systems used by employees.

Eventually an administrator (and part-time HR person) shows up with the HR and benefits paperwork for Charlie to fill out. He's not sure about training, though, and he doesn't know about getting Charlie access. The administrator offers his manager's mobile number so

Charlie can get the lay of the land. Charlie tries, but it rolls to voicemail.

What is Onboarding?

Quite simply, onboarding is the process of bringing a new hire (or contractor) into your company and making them as effective and comfortable as possible. Onboarding involves more than just your new employee's first day and far more than helping him/her with the legal and benefits paperwork.

Why does onboarding matter?

1. **Productivity**. Almost all startups are resource starved, so you want your new hire to get up to speed as quickly as possible and start adding value.

2. **Tenure**. You want your new hire to feel welcome and happy about the decision to join your startup.

A study by Aberdeen Group suggests that 86% of new hires aren't fully committed to a new job for the first six months and make a decision to stay with a company long-term during that time.

Replacing employees is *expensive*! A study by The Society for Human Resource Management estimated that it cost six to nine months of an employee's salary to find and train a replacement. For a $100,000 person, you're talking $60,000 to $90,000!

Don't waste the money and time that you spent recruiting and training your new employee only to see them walk out the door based on a horrible first impression.

A great onboarding process includes a proper welcome, orienting the employee with systems and new people, a welcoming space, and some training on how you operate.

Obviously, the degree and depth of your onboarding process depends entirely on the stage of development of your startup. You won't have a complicated onboarding process if your startup only has five people in it. As your company grows, and your processes and structure get more complex, your onboarding process needs to grow to match.

Setting Your Onboarding Goals

While everyone in the startup is running at hyper speed, onboarding has a few attainable goals:

- Getting the new employee up to speed
- Getting them to stick
- Helping them socially adapt and integrate to the company and culture

Current employees are often thrilled to have a new team member come on board, to grow the company and help lighten the work load, but they often have a hard time slowing down enough to really bring on a new team member effectively. In some cases, the earliest employees have a subconscious feeling that new employees should have to "find their way" in much the same way that they did in the early days.

It's ironic of course—stressed, overworked managers and team members want new hires to come up to speed and contribute as fast as possible. As a result, they may even resist effective onboarding because they "don't have time."

Because of this, it is important as a leader to lay out to the team what you need from them to set up an effective onboarding process.

- Establish goals with the management team, and each of the functional teams.

- Be welcoming, helping the new employee learn the social norms.

- Bring the new employee up to speed with systems, hardware, software, and a work space prepared.

- Train the new employee on your company, customers, products, and market.

- Have the employee's manager lay out their expectations for performance over time.

You would also like all of that to happen as quickly as possible, so the new hire can contribute meaningfully and take some of the workload off the current staff.

Best Practices

Many times, onboarding efforts are led by HR, and are therefore more administrative in nature. Though paperwork and benefits are necessary tasks, they should not be the crux of their first hours.

Onboarding includes setting up meetings with peers or other key employees ahead of time. It includes:

- Who will greet them on their first day?

- Who gives them a tour of the office, the kitchen, the bathrooms

- Is their desk or office area clean and ready for them?

- What kind of computer and monitor do they get and is it ready for them?

- Is their email set up?

- Have you ordered their business cards?

- Do they have system access for important business systems, email, file access, Jira?

- Where do they find the org chart or list of employees?

- Are there events they should know about, both large (summer outing) and small (Friday catered lunch)?

- What are the expectations of their manager, how do they get communicated?

- Does someone announce new hires by email or Slack?

Developing a full cycle "hiring system" will take work and thought. You may not feel like you have the time for it, but hopefully you see that all of these pieces are necessary to truly scale your team with A players. Again, they key is to keep process light, but to document it.

Interview with Rob Chesney, COO, Trunk Club

Rob Chesney was COO of Trunk Club and was instrumental in growing the business to over 1,500 people before its sale to Nordstrom for over $350 million. He was previously an executive at eBay.

Rob Kornblum:
Tell me a little bit more about Trunk Club when you joined, the scale of the business when you started, and after you guys sold it.

Rob Chesney:
I joined in 2011. The company had just raised its Series A. The scale of the company—we were doing about $5 to $7 million of revenue annually. [We] had about 30 people, but I'd say at least 15 of those people were sales people. The core operating team was quite small.

I was hired in as the COO and essentially, Brian and I decided to divide and conquer. He was going to build our sales team, which we knew would be quite large—ended up being a 700-person sales team—and really run merchandising. I was tasked with figuring out how to build our technology platform, our marketing strategy and capabilities, and really scale ops.

Because you guys had physical inventory you need to package up and all the rest of that, right? You were moving product.

Yes, it looked like what they call omnichannel today. We did a bunch more e-commerce early on; we shipped inventory out to consumers across the country. Over time, we also opened physical locations. We bought inventory in advance, warehoused it, sold it at a margin, dealt with returns, all that good stuff.

What was the total company size when you guys sold it?

Between 2011 and when we sold it, which was the summer of 2015, we went from $5 million in annualized revenues to [over] $100 million. Everything after that is non-public, but I think it's gone [up] two to three times from there since then.

We went from a 30-person team to over 1,500 people [with] 600 or 700 sales people. We had a relatively large ops team doing fulfillment and logistics, so lower-cost employees, warehouse-type stuff, which might have been another 400. The rest of the team was maybe [300].

That's a lot of scale.

Our philosophy, we talked about there being certain capabilities you want to invest ahead of the curve, [on the curve, and] behind the curve.

As a consumer business, knowing that we would raise our Series B 18 months [after our Series A], we needed to figure out customer acquisition. We invested way more in a data platform to highlight how our funnel was working, how our [customer] acquisition was going. We hired out more people there upfront (engineers). Things that were on the curve were much more sales, and support, and CS capabilities...behind the curve was investment in things like warehouse technology and ops technology. Stuff that was really important long-term and that scales, but was not the thing to get us from A to B, you know?

Job one was organizing a set of strategic priorities and then hiring to build these capabilities. We had no technology or marketing team in place, really. Our technology team, for example, was two outsourced engineers and one or two junior people in-house. It was like starting from scratch.

One of the things that I liken it to, right or wrong, is a process like MVP from a product perspective, like minimally viable. You need process, but you only need enough for where you are. You got really good at finding people, [then] processing them through and figuring out who was going to be successful, [then] onboarding. Talk to me about building up some of those processes, especially as an early-stage business.

Well, I think we knew a couple of things and then we made a lot of mistakes...we tried to adapt as we were learning from our mistakes. Because we were hiring so fast, we definitely were not perfect.

I think we made a commitment to never use a recruiter. We actually ended up building our own internal recruiting resource. We could not stomach the cost. I think our comfort level with doing that [in-house] was driven by the fact that we knew we were going to hire relatively large operational and sales teams. That would be a very tough decision for a company scaling from 12 to 18 people versus scaling from 30 to 300.

Really the hard part of hiring is managers just don't have time to run that process effectively. So, garbage in, garbage out, or bottlenecks in timing. A lot of young managers, in particular, have never hired at scale or gone in a rapid growth business...like I used to describe to my Head of Engineering. He would say, "I don't have time!" I would respond, "You can never stop recruiting. You always have to allocate some portion of time because it's a death spiral [in terms of pipeline]." You're two people down, you're working harder to cover the gap of those two people, so you spend even less time on recruiting...

And you're three people down.

Yeah, then someone leaves, and things blow up. We talked a lot about this internally about how quickly we were trying to scale, how rapidly we were trying to grow. I think we counter-balanced that with a lot of, I guess, philosophical cultural-level discussions around performance.

You're never going to hire perfectly. You end up [sometimes] with people who are somewhat mediocre, and managers end up disproportionally spending their time with poor performers. Your best people are the most alienated [when that happens].

We were just really on top of [making] people understand that it's okay that not every hire works out. Usually the people who aren't working out, they know it's not working out for them either. Just be good about how you manage that process, be forthright, have a clear way you do it. No one should ever be surprised.

I used to educate all these young managers on...a fair process for how to manage performance, how to do it quickly, and how to turn your gut instincts about someone's performance into a process that actually manages them inwards, upwards, or out relatively quickly. Young managers feel a lot of ownership over this person that they hired, and they don't want to admit that they made a mistake, so they spend a lot of time rehabbing them, and pushing them, and marginalizing their role, and letting them be a toxic influence on the org just to protect themselves. But when you're scaling from 30 people to 500 people, you can't wake up one day with 150 B players.

No, for sure. Back to the pipeline part because it's actually one of the book "secrets". How much did time you encourage your Head of Engineering to spend recruiting?

Off-the-cuff, I probably talked about 20% of the time should be recruiting. (That answer changed, by the way, at different points.) And our engineering team doesn't scale anywhere near our sales and other teams. It went from a team of nothing to a team of across all data, analytics functions; it was probably 90 or so people.

But early on, [we] were adding two or three good engineers every couple of months. I was like, "Hey, this should be 20% of your time." It wouldn't surprise me if he spent 30 to 50% of his time recruiting [when he had a larger team].

To find high-quality people just takes time and it takes a network. For him, it wasn't such a mass volume of people that we needed some third-party software solution. I just told him to develop a networking best practice. Keep a spreadsheet or keep a list of people.

For me, [the] best time to recruit was when you were not recruiting... when you could invite someone over, show them your business, ask for their advice, get their perspective, get them engaged in the business or whatever; then just by having them exposed to the business, they're either excited about it or not. You can sell them from there.

I think it's much better to have that when there's not a lot of strings attached [or a job req posted]. So then when the day comes and you say, "Hey look, we're filling this role. I've gotten to know you, you've gotten to know our business." It's a networking practice, you know?

The first time you reach out to them can't be the time that you want them to sign on the dotted line, it has to be you're building an authentic relationship. In Chicago, there's a lot of [good] talent, but they're not in places you would typically find them, but if you build a relationship and get them excited, it can work. They're really loyal, it's hard to dig them out...It was an interesting place to [recruit].

In [Silicon] Valley, everyone knows they're being recruited all the time and they know they're a highly liquid and mobile workforce. Coming here from the Bay Area, the tactics ended up looking really quite different.

Yeah, really different. One other process you guys must have been good at is onboarding. Tell me a little bit about some of the things you did.

I think we figured out some things that made us good, but I'm not sure that we were good at every stage...we used to describe those first 50 people in the company as [being able to handle a]

"No-look pass." These people understand the strategy, the core values of the company, the big priorities at any given moment. As soon as you go over that 100-person mark, it's surprising how quickly onboarding or communication channels just don't scale.

I think onboarding is a good example. I think those are the people who feel it first, you're looking at them like, "Don't you get it?" And they're like, "I have no idea what this company's about [or] how things work. I don't know who to go to for x, y, and z." I think we had moments in our evolution where we're like, "Oh, shit. We don't have the right kind of processes in place."

In sales, they did a two to four-week trial where they were expected to be in the office. Even if they were working full-time at a job, they would come in evenings and "do the job." In partnership with another experienced sales person, they would be expected to bring in their own customers and serve them, call people on the phone, answer email, do all these things.

It was one part, like a qualitative assessment; can our sales people interact with our customers? Do they have the energy to do [this job]? And secondly, more objectively, can they actually generate outcomes? Usually at the end of those trials, employees sometimes opted out because they just didn't feel like it was the right fit for them, or we chose that they were not the right people. It was this nice little weeding mechanism, a two-way test drive.

And then once an employee decided that they wanted to join the company, we had a month-long training program set up...a lot of practical, on-the-job, with a small team; we had actual training organizations within our sales organization that were explicitly focused on the core capabilities required for the job...or every month, we would have a new class that onboarded. We would sit there and we would tell our own versions of the origin story of the business. They would ask us questions about our careers and our backgrounds.

We used moments like this, to communicate-

The values, and the mission, and that kind of thing.

Yeah...just authentically delivered from all of our perspectives, like what we like, what we don't like...Some of our best performing sales people we had to let go [because] it's not enough just to be good at this job from a sales performance perspective. You're promoted, basically, on the feedback of your peers, not just based on objective outcomes. We encouraged a lot of transparency and a lot of humility. In an organization where you're building sales people, how do you build a competitive performance or a sales team that still has a culture of team togetherness?

Engineering [was] almost the opposite end of the spectrum. The onboarding there was totally tailored and designed by that team; you paired with people, you did rotation for a certain period of time, they had intense peer review processes...these [guys and girls] would do live, in-person small group 360-feedback sessions. "Here's three things that I love. Here's three things that I think you should work on." I sat in on a handful of these. They were amazing! I think people pulled punches in terms of politeness but not topics. I really loved that process and they were very good about feedback and reviews, and so that's how they weeded through who's thriving and growing here, and who needs to be worked out of the organization.

And how did the non-sales teams communicate? You talked about communicating values and mission?

Maybe not as well, but I think they were much smaller teams and much easier in some ways. We ended up having multiple layers of communication. We had full-company meetings where we learned very quickly we could only talk about the most high-level good or bad news or key messages. In much smaller group team meetings, you could still have more of a nuanced conversation about people, things that are [or aren't] going well, things that we need to work on.

I want to go further on that because it's one of the really interesting million-dollar questions. There's no right answer but there's strongly held opinions on very opposite sides. One group of founders saying, "Absolutely, positively, hire for culture," and another group saying, "Actually, those words, 'hire for culture' or 'culture fit' really create homogenous organizations and is code word for bias, etc.," who believe much more that culture comes from the bottom-up rather than the top-down. I'm curious where you fall on that spectrum.

At our all-hands where we talked about some of those onboarding sessions, culture was one of the things I talked about the most, "Look, I know companies talk a lot about culture and what it means to them. But if I walked around this room with 25 people and handed out a slip of paper [to write down] what culture means to you, we'd have wildly divergent opinions...so let me tell you a little bit about what I've learned about culture and what I think it means in an organization like ours."

To me, culture means being around a group of people who inspire you every day. Have you ever gone to a job where based on the environment, the culture of the company, or the people you're working with, you almost don't want to go to work that day? You're just so miserable [and] frustrated, you're white-knuckling it in the parking lot...That, to me, is a sign that there's something wrong, culturally, with that company.

To me, we should be hiring a group of people who may or may not be your best friend at the end of the day, but they push you. Maybe they're people who are really good at their jobs [or] very collaborative and very friendly. Maybe they're people who are doing inspiring things in their lives outside of work [or] supporting loved ones. Maybe they're going to school on the side.... You want to be surrounded by a group of people that are motivating and inspiring and not toxic, people who are not anti-team culture.

It's a very amorphous definition, but...when I see HR teams in particular turn culture into programs, I find they almost always miss the mark. It is always about [birthday parties or anniversary gifts, like], "Why don't we do company-sponsored one-on-one lunches, so you can meet people across the company?" I think they fuck it up. Not just that that stuff is bad, but it's like that's not what [culture] is. As a manager, make sure your team has a group of people where they don't have to be [the] same.

One of my hiring tips I've tried to share with other people is if someone makes you uncomfortable, it doesn't mean they're a bad hire. Quite often, the [people who make you] uncomfortable...like, "This person is 180-degrees different from me," they can actually be really additive to culture.

I think the difference isn't who's right or who's wrong, hire-for-culture not hire-for-culture; I think what's wrong is that statement... What is the culture you're trying to create? And then if you can really define it in terms that make sense, I think, at a more detailed level, then absolutely hire for culture or fire for lack of it...I guess my caveat would be, how inclusive and diverse that definition can be is very different than what I think what I hear HR people (or inexperienced managers and founders) talk about culture. It isn't free snacks or birthday parties.

Yeah, their version of "fit" is, "Someone I'm comfortable with," right? That's where you get these narrow, narrow definitions.

So taking that a step further, when you guys built executive teams [from] Senior Managers all the way up to VPs, tell me a little bit more about your best advice regarding culture, because you've got people who've got 10+ years of experience and are going to bring that experience in. How does that translates into reinforcing or even changing your culture?

Yeah, I think I definitely made some mistakes in this one.

We had a relatively lean executive team. In our company, even when we were over 1,000 people, the key operational execs [were] maybe a team of 10. So we didn't build out a platoon of VPs and either over-hire or over-promote people. But when I think about execs, high-quality hires, anyone we brought in at Director or VP or above, they were really important hires culturally and to the operation of the business.

Our philosophy was to be hyper-decentralized. We prioritized speed over top-down decision making. Now, it was organized [with] high-level KPIs and all the right meetings, but we really tried to eliminate all the tax of reporting up through organizations that control decision-making at the very top...wherever possible.

When we hired people into those roles, they had to hit the ground running. It varies a little bit by function, but I used to describe the people hiring in these areas. [To] simplify it, I said, "There's two things we really care about: your actual hard skill set, like can you do the job we're actually asking you to do? [And will you thrive in a dynamic, decentralized culture where people make their own mistakes and learn from them?]" [In] most cases, based on really solid third-party background checking, good onboarding hiring interview process, I think you can get pretty accurate on hard skills. I didn't often feel we were getting surprised too often.

I described [the second part of the equation] as a psychographic profile. "Hey, we have an organization with a relatively distinct and decentralized culture that's running a certain type of race, not a slow arc. Our internal operating philosophies and values are really important to us... We're trying to grow from $10 million in revenue to $200 million in revenue. We're trying to scale this fast. We're not going on a slow arc here, we're going fast. We like to empower our people to make decisions, build their own teams...we're not fearful of mistakes but we're humble about when we are wrong and we're curious about what we learn from it."

[Then] say, "Will you thrive in that environment?" They all say, "Yes." Unfortunately...you put people into a relatively unstructured, fast-moving environment where key decision-making and execution is being pushed down to them and it's lean...Some people thrive and just immediately take off, and some people just, for whatever reason, stall out.

[We could get smarter] about tracking [success] in terms of what culture did they come from? What size of company? What kind of role did they have? Where did they fit in? Unfortunately, on that dimension, it ends up being a quick workout on the other side once they're in.

Sure. [When you made the] executive hires, how did you integrate the team, to make sure that there was trust built?

We didn't do a ton of them. I think one of the mistakes companies make growing an early start-up is they bring in layers on top of really highly motivated, talented young people. My personal philosophy was...to really push and promote from within and put people in stretch roles. But if I'm honest, you can't have your whole functional leadership team with people in stretch roles, though the right people could be set up for the right challenge.

[So] back to this question of do they actually thrive in this unstructured, fast-moving, decentralized environment? The intersection of those two things...we started having Directors or VPs [candidates]...work on a case. We took a real problem that was related to the area they were going to come in and work on. They weren't the most pointed questions..."All right. You're going to come in and manage operations. Lay out your 90-day plan."

Rather than just get some off-the-cuff philosophical, "how I'd approach my first 90 days," we actually said, "Hey, why don't you take a couple of weeks to cross-functionally interview your team or our finance team for whatever data you'd like to see...to whoever you want? You have unfettered access to our business."

We told them, "It's not about getting to a right answer or doing 1,000 hours of homework. Just go get the gist of it and then come back and present it to us." Man, these people worked.

And you wanted to see how they would think?

It was amazing. Could they actually convert what they were saying into what they were doing? The added bonus was we got so much great feedback that they collaborated with. If we gave them a finance analyst to go run queries for them and they treated the finance analyst like shit, we had a great red flag.

It was the experiential interview on steroids?

Totally. [They] had to organize their thinking into cogent output, so you got this great view of 1,000-foot operating level interacting with analysts, and pulling data...then this 30,000-foot view which is can they roll it up into something that's digestible and understandable?

We would have conversations with three candidates that were down to our final three candidates in a role, and they were so close, and we would debate about marginal differences; they would spread out across a continuum like you wouldn't believe. It was so clarifying on so many dimensions. That ended up being our go-to.

One thing that I want... either from Trunk Club or your investor experience, give me your single biggest tip for new CEOs, for hiring and culture.

One is understanding the difference between people's skillsets and whether they'll actually thrive in your organization and your culture. I advise them that they can get very good at one; they'll bat 50% on the second category... if for their first 12 hires they've hired three or four people that don't fit in that second category, they will be on their way to building a mediocre team. You will definitely be wrong [when hiring, so] here's how you have to deal with it on the other end; rapidly get out the people who aren't the right fit or the right performance characteristics.

It's not just about hiring correctly [but] understanding where your bias and your mistakes are most likely to show up. Make sure you're evaluating employees very quickly upon their arrival, whether they're actually working the way you think they're working. Make sure you have as airtight a process on the backend [as on the front end], to figure out whether someone's actually working out or not, and how to deal with it.

That's fantastic. You think that's what, a 30 to 90-day winnowing?

Look, this is a less objective process, granted, but your gut as a manager is telling you within 30 days whether you made the right hiring move. I want to see people move off your teams; it's a sign of a healthy start-up, but you substantiate it on a review process. You don't do it on ad hoc feedback...We all know it as managers, [the difference] between something that is marginal performance improvement that they need to work on and something fundamental, either performance or culture.

[Even] if it's only 30 days in, you sit down with that person and you say, "Look, this is not going to be an easy conversation. I've got this feedback, and I think we have a fundamental issue here. I'm concerned about our ability to turn this around, but I wanted to share it with you. If we can't figure it out in the next 30 days, I'm worried that it's not going to end up in a good place." It's not like babying the feedback; transparency is not emotionally driven.

Fantastic; it's like the chapter 'Everything Breaks at 100.' You talked a little bit about the need for changing communication at a certain scale and for whatever reason, people have coalesced around this 100. There's no magic to that number. What were some of the things that you found needed change, and how did you guys change them?

It used to be very clear and easy for us to do an all-hands and communicate a lot and at all levels. The subject matter could be, "Rah rah rah, didn't we do great hitting our numbers? Let's look at this feature we launched and let's look at a Gantt chart of where our product roadmap is going." You can do that in a 30-person team [or] 50-person team.

You start getting north of 100, even if they're in the same location, the content can't be that nuanced or [detailed]. You end up having to move your messaging higher. We started having 500-person all-hands... "Rah rah, mission". Then we realized we needed to break down this team communication into smaller team communications. That worked really well.

It started with engineering because that was the obvious place but we did sprint reviews every two weeks across every function. Every team was running a sprint cadence where they had one meeting on the calendar every two weeks that told them everything that they were working on.

Multiple geographies got really hard. We tried to teleconference, to videoconference, and realized very quickly we need to actually go on the road as an executive team and touch these offices [in-person] at some cadence and frequency... where they were seeing and hearing from us in-person and do something that was a little less scalable.

Then just creating a fun but substantive monthly newsletter; each team wrote their own. We didn't do every team every month, but we would pick two or three teams [who] would write a four or five-paragraph blurb...we got 50% feedback that people loved it and we got 50% feedback like, "Why the hell are we doing this? No one reads this stuff." I think we ran out of ideas at some of that level.

Working with Recruiters

Even if you build a strong pipeline, and a great hiring system, there will be times in your startup's hiring lifecycle that require working with recruiters.

Different Types of Recruiters

The first thing to understand about recruiters is that there are basically two different types of recruiters: retained and contingent. They function very differently and most of the time, they operate under completely different firms. (Occasionally, however, a firm may do both, and it is very important to distinguish between the types of arrangements.)

Retained recruiters, often called executive search firms, get paid their fees regardless of the success of the search. These retainer fees are typically one-third of the expected cash compensation of the hired executive, plus the expenses of the search process. For example, if you are hiring a VP of Marketing with an expected base of $200,000 and an expected (on plan) bonus of $100,000, the search firm retainer will be $100,000.

The retainer fees are often paid out over time. Common payment terms are one-third per month over three months. Another model is two-thirds over the first two months, and then the last third upon completion of the search. (Remember that this last payment is not contingent, you have to pay it.)

Because of the magnitude of the fees, and because the firm gets paid regardless of the success, most CEOs and boards only choose to hire retained search firms for executive-level hires. Most of the time, this is for C-level hires or VP/SVP who will report to the CEO.

Contingent Search

The other main type of search firm is a contingent search firm. A contingent firm only gets paid if you hire the candidate that they submit to you. Generally speaking, the fees for contingent search are lower than for retained searches (20% to 25% of the total expected compensation).

The idea of contingent search is appealing—they only get paid if you hire their candidate. Because of this appeal, sometimes you will see inexperienced hiring managers and CEOs use a contingent firm when they should hire a retained firm.

There are a few significant challenges with contingent search firms. Because the contingent firm is often competing with other contingent firms, and with company-sourced candidates, they often "race" to submit candidates in order to try to get their fee. (If they wait to interview and vet the candidate, they might lose out to other firms. They will have done a bunch of work for no money). As a result, contingent searches can result in lower quality candidates, lower fit for the position, or limited due diligence on candidates.

Less scrupulous contingent firms will also sometimes submit candidates for other openings, or mid-level roles that they expect you will be hiring for, even without a specific contract. They do this in the hope that, if you hire "their" candidate down the line, they can extract a fee from you. Be careful about this practice. Make sure you do some reference checks on the search firm; call their clients and ask about the process and the integrity of the firm. Be sure not to accept other resumés without a very clear understanding of the firm's expectations regarding those candidates.

In terms of payment, contingent fees are payable upon completion of the search.

What Does a Search Firm Do?

Depending on whether you work with a retained search firm or a contingency firm, search firms can assist with all parts of the recruiting process:

- Developing a position description
- Benchmarking the proposed salary
- Sourcing candidates
- Interviewing and screening, background and other reference checks
- Negotiating with the final selected candidate

Once the position description and compensation are set, your interaction begins.

The firm will ask you for a list of prior work experience and background of your ideal candidate. They will ask you for a list of companies that your perfect company would work for, which will probably be 10 to 20 companies long. If you're an enterprise software startup, maybe your list would include large companies like Oracle, Microsoft, or Salesforce; recent startups might include companies such as Workday, LogMeIn, Box, etc.

The search firm will then locate initial or "trial" candidates to see if they are on the right track. Expect to see, review, and give feedback on resumés or LinkedIn profiles of a handful of candidates.

After the specification is locked in, the search firm will start to locate, speak with, vet, and then present candidates for the role.

One of the most important parts of this process is to make sure the search firm knows how to "sell" your startup to candidates. A candidate will need to understand why they should consider leaving their current position to join a new company that they have never heard of; this is easier if you have developed a robust employer brand. Remember that you are selling your founders, your vision for market domination, your funding and VCs, and your culture.

Once you meet candidates for interviews, and move toward making an offer, it is important to have a frank conversation with the search firm about who will be doing what to present and negotiate the offer. The search firm will very much want to be the intermediary, but that is not always the best bet.

Process and Time Line

Working with recruiters takes time and is not a "silver bullet" to all your recruiting woes or challenges. You definitely need to allocate enough time to the process so the recruiting firm gets to know you and your company well enough to effectively "sell" you to the candidates. But if you choose good recruiters and are realistic about your requirements and the salaries, many companies find success this way.

The recruiting firm will work with you to put together a professional-sounding "position description" (PD) that describes the role, the requirements, and your startup. They send this document to interested candidates after they contact them. The process of creating the PD takes a few weeks of meeting you, getting to know your culture, and then some back-and-forth with you.

The firm also creates a target list of companies from which you would pull your ideal candidates. This helps them to begin targeting through their own database and networking efforts, LinkedIn, and other online tools like DiscoverOrg.

Once they find a few possible candidates, they will send you those for review to see if they are on the right track, or off base, before they really begin generating lists of possible candidates. This step is quite important, because the search firm's understanding of what you are looking for might be off base by a little or maybe by a lot. It is essential to "course correct" their efforts before they get too far into the search, or you will both waste a lot of time.

The other reason to review these first few candidates is to help you determine what background elements and cultural elements *really* matter to you for this role. In my experience, hiring managers and executives generally put together a long list of "nice to have" attributes for a role, but a few of these matter the most. Often times, you won't know which ones matter the most until you start the sorting process, placing candidates into the "Yes" and the "No" piles, which will reveal some must-haves and must-not-haves for your position description.

You may want to change the PD based on that new understanding. At a minimum, make sure your most important criteria are understood by the search firm team. They will phone and email a long list of candidates to gauge their interest, send the PD, and begin screening candidates before sending any to you.

Once you start meeting with candidates, and are seeing some good to great fits, the process should flow basically like your normal interview and hiring process.

Guarantees

Due to the size of the fees, tens to hundreds of thousands of dollars, search contracts sometimes have a negotiable "guarantee", which protects the hiring company if the candidate turns out to be a poor fit who leaves or is fired soon after starting. The existence of a guarantee provision, and its many elements, are negotiable.

Basically, if you terminate the employee in the first 90 days (sometimes longer), the search firm will repeat the search for you. Rarely will you actually get money back from them.

Contract and In-House Recruiters

In addition to retained and contingent search firms, startups that are scaling rapidly will sometimes bring in a "contract recruiter" to help locate talent. Contract recruiters basically act like internal employees who get paid hourly, although there can be other compensation arrangements as well.

Contract recruiters can reduce a lot of the legwork for hiring managers by identifying candidates, doing an initial screen, and representing the company. However, quality can really vary, so make sure that you bring in really good people who are trained exceptionally well. Remember, they are representing you.

As you really start to scale, you will probably hire in-house recruiters as part of your full-time team. One of the metrics to look for, as you contemplate hiring an in-house recruiter, is repeatability: 'How many of the same position type will we hire this year?'

For example, if you are hiring five sales people with similar requirements, or 10 developers, then it may make sense to hire someone in-house. The specifications for the roles will be similar; the research, pipeline, and key learnings are common and shareable. When that is true, in-house recruiters make sense.

Interview with Jothy Rosenberg, Founder & CEO of Dover Microsystems

Jothy Rosenberg is a nine-time entrepreneur with two exits valued over $100 million. Dover Microsystems, a revolutionary cybersecurity company, is his most recent startup. [Disclosure: I am an advisor to Dover].

Rob Kornblum:
Jothy, tell me about building your team at Dover.

Jothy Rosenberg: In building the initial team at Dover, we have followed a very strict policy of hiring no strangers. [Our initial team] are all people that I've worked with before, at least once... in some cases, it's five times. Or someone you really trust is strongly recommending someone, they are not [really] a stranger.

What you end up with is a group of people that completely trust each other to do their job. No one can cover for anyone else because everyone's got 200% of what they can handle... I wouldn't say we're a well-oiled machine, but we're very efficient. There's no room for people that aren't efficient or competent. People are still able to have fun. They joke around, but they work really hard. The extension of this when we sort of all ran out of—

Of the people you knew.

Yeah, of the people we knew that were moveable. Then the next extension of that was the best recruiter I've ever known. She came in initially [in '89] as a contract recruiter to my very first startup out in Sunnyvale. She's built four other teams for me. She wants to help us build the team to 50 people. Anybody in the company who started to interact with her says, "This is different. I've never had a recruiter [who] does this." She really asks incredibly detailed questions. Then she says, "Okay, now we're going to do some fit testing. Am I hitting the mark?"

The first hire we were going to make, she came back with a spreadsheet of 2,000 names that she had already filtered down. Then she further highlighted the ones that she thought were a good fit. The first step was, go through these resumés, and then we'll have an hour-long meeting. [She asks] "tell me what looks good and what doesn't from the resumés. Then I'm going to take the ones that do look good, or I'm going to go back and get some more, and I'm going to phone screen."

[After phone screening,] she came back and said, "I've got two really good ones." We picked the one that sounded the best. He came in on a Friday, and then that was just meeting a couple people. Then he came back the following Thursday for a full round of interviews, and we made him an offer on the spot and didn't want him to leave the building.

Right. What [are] the tricks in working with [a recruiter], in terms of having her represent the company in the way that you want and having her technical enough to do some of those?

Well, first of all, [you have to have a recruiter you trust.] I knew it was worth an investment of a significant amount of time to treat her like she was already an employee. She needed to understand the company, the product, the team, the market. She does not have any computer science training, but she's been around this industry. She also knows what kind of things motivate sales people, marketing people, engineering people... She's able to have the tough love conversation about compensation: "That company paid you that much? You won't get that anywhere else. You think that much equity is reasonable? Think about how much this company's going to be worth." She will just weed out a few [through pattern matching] and lots of experience.

If you didn't have that relationship that dates back to '89, or you're talking to a first-time founder who's kind of getting to this regular scale past the people we know, what are the magic bullets there?

Yeah. I mean, if you're only hiring one or two people a quarter, then you can probably do it yourself.

In the hiring realm, what are some of the other things that you look for culturally? As an example, [how do you] draw on that bad experience and say, "We're screening out this or that"?

Well, I like to say that there's an imaginary sign over the company door that says, "No bozos allowed." You hire slowly and you fire quickly. If somebody isn't working out, it's better for them and better for you if you say, "Whoops, made a mistake."

Even though we're small, we have a pretty formal process. First of all, I make sure everybody is reminded (or learn) how to do behavioral interviewing. You can't really learn very much about people [through traditional interviews.] Interviewing is a completely artificial substitute for working every day.

Likeability is too big a part of it, right? Watch out for the person that dominates the conversation. They have to be able to listen and tell you things. [Don't ask the candidate] questions from their resumé that are already there. Ask them, "Hey, when you were in this role at this company, and you were responsible for this project. How big was the team? Were you in charge? What went really well or badly?" You want to get people to tell stories. It's the only way you can try to imagine how they do their job, and that's your goal is to figure out how they do the job, not how well they interview because they'll never interview with you again.

That makes sense. You talk about a formal process. When did you put that formal process into place?

Right away, when I put the very first team together, which was eight of us. We decided to bring in numbers nine and 10. We said, "Now is when we have this formal process. Here's who we're looking for, and there's a req that we all agree to." Someone will say, "You forgot about this." That's the purpose of circulating the req. Whoever's taking the lead is trying to get candidates, but before they come in, [the interview team decides] who's going to cover what so that you're not all asking the same questions.

I don't believe it's healthy or realistic for people go through eight hours of interviews...Try to make it convenient for everybody, but a couple half days. Don't be afraid of having two-on-one interviews that allow some playing off of each other. While one's asking a question, the other's formulating their next question, which is better because you want to be fully listening to the person and not looking down and thinking of the next question while they're answering your previous question.

Also, very, very important. In the middle of the interview day, somebody can say to the next interviewer, "I forgot to ask about this," or "I got a funny feeling about this. Could you probe on that?" Then the final thing is, while it's totally fresh in everyone's mind on that same day, get the whole team together. Don't allow people to do thumbs up, thumbs down. That's the objective answer for later, but ask people based on the behavioral interviews that you did, what were the good things and worrisome things that you saw, relative to what we're looking for?

Depending on how things went, I'm usually at the end [of the schedule]. I might be in sell mode, or I might want to find out a little bit more about how they tick. What do they do when they're not at work, etc.

I'm looking for culture fit, which I do believe in. For example, if this person has never worked in a startup, and you're still within the first 25 people, that might be a concern. That might be hard for them to fit in because you don't want somebody to say, "Well, no, that's not my job." Nobody [should] ever say that in a startup.

Right.

I want as much cultural diversity as possible in culture with the sort of normal meaning, but within our little four walls, I don't want somebody that's got a sour attitude. It's hard enough [doing a startup]. You kind of need people that are pretty optimistic, pretty flexible.

I know all you modern guys call it "pivoting", but we used to call it "bobbing and weaving". When you're bobbing and weaving, your job as the CEO is to make sure everybody's aligned and that they understand what the recent change is and why.

You don't want people to say, "Well, a week ago you told me to do this, and now you're telling me to do that." I'm looking for those kinds of things that say, 'Are they going to be able to deal with [being in a startup with occasional setbacks]?' That's what I'm trying to figure out.

Last question: what do you feel like you know now about hiring that you wish you knew in your earlier startups?

Well, it took me until startup three or four to realize that I needed a recruiter. It's like, how many [people] leave college knowing that it's really important to maintain these friendships? It took me fifteen years, maybe. Ever since then, if we had a good connection, no matter when or where, I'm going to keep in touch with that person and value that connection. For any number of reasons that you may not be able to predict. I was certainly guilty of that with Mary. You can't lose track of any of these good people that worked at any of your companies because the top 5%, you're going to want to try to work with again.

[It] was not until I was pretty far along, probably about age 35, before I had even heard the term "behavioral interview". Before that, it was like asking these things where they could just give you an answer that's already in the resumé. It's such a complete waste of time.

I don't think I even got the, "Don't hire strangers" until startup number eight and nine. That's probably the most valuable piece of [advice] I could give...you're a little bit older, more experienced, so that you have these great connections that you've built up. Then you reach back out to them.

In the case of this company, there were so many miracles or coincidences where just the person I needed was right then looking. Yeah, amazing. The stars were aligned for getting this one going.

When You Have to Fire People

One of the most challenging times for a startup CEO is having to terminate someone.

Any number of situations could cause this, but two are most common: (a) having to quickly remove a bad hire and (b) when the business scales past the person's capabilities.

Most often, poor hires are good people who just don't fit into what you are trying to get done. It could be that they are used to more support in a larger company, or that their skills might translate better for your startup if you were in a different phase.

It's not always clear *why* it is not working, but your gut tells you that it is not working. Trust your gut, but then verify. It's important to verify so that you can speak with the employee, and make sure you don't make the same hiring mistake again.

Often, founders will wait to remove a bad fit because they know the person and they don't want to rock the boat, or because they hope that things will work out. Sometimes it does and changing the person's role changes his performance.

Rob Chesney, COO of Trunk Club, said (in his interview) that less experienced managers can feel "over-invested" in a particular hire. That manifests itself by trying to coach and remediate a bad hire beyond what makes sense. They feel "invested" in the new hire. While that is admirable and honorable, it often doesn't make business sense in a fast moving startup.

When everyone is running a million miles an hour, it can feel crazy to *remove* someone from the company and try to stretch their workload among everyone else. But it almost always makes sense to do that because the rest of your team is being dragged down, not elevated, by the low performer.

One of the most important considerations in termination is that people should not be surprised to be fired. If you sense that an employee is at risk, don't delay having a frank discussion with him about that, so he knows how to improve performance through objective criteria. Be crystal clear, without being mean. "John, there is currently a problem with your performance, and here is what you need to do to fix it." Your company has far too much to accomplish for people to not be on the same page and performing well.

Once the at-risk person understands and acknowledges the problems, make a plan to meet with them with frequently (assuming that they report to you). Don't just depend on your normal check in cycle, or the standups, to get a sense of what they are working on.

Keeping closer tabs will enable you to see their progress, or lack thereof, against the performance plan.

If the issue is fit and attitude, be honest and cite examples. Give them a chance to correct the behavior, but know in your heart that these things rarely work out. Every founder who has spoken to me about hiring and team building has told me the same thing. If anything, they waited too long to move on a problem hire.

It's hard for a mission-driven founder, especially a person with empathy, to look someone in the eye and tell them that you are terminating them. Put yourself in their shoes and be honest.

Often with executives or team leaders, the business has scaled past the employee. This case is perhaps more challenging, because of your great sense of loyalty to the executive for helping you build the business to this point. But most CEOs I have spoken with, including Amy Errett, Founder & CEO of Madison Reed (interview to follow), that the employee and the manager usually know that it isn't really working anymore.

With an executive or team lead who helped you build the business to this point, you should probably be able to assist them in landing something in a more appropriate stage company. If you have investors, they may well know portfolio companies of theirs who are looking. That was certainly the case for Steve Hafner, Founder & CEO of Kayak (a prior interview). Kayak's VCs helped place Kayak execs who were looking for an earlier stage opportunity.

Regardless of the circumstance, one additional challenge you will face is around what to tell the rest of the employees. On the one hand, you want to be as open and upfront as possible with the remaining employees. Some of them may worry about their own performance, or the company's future.

On the other hand, you may face legal liability for being transparent. Be sure to check with a labor attorney to understand what you can and cannot share and how best to phrase things.

Interview with Amy Errett, Founder & CEO, Madison Reed

Amy Errett founded and leads Madison Reed, a high-growth eCommerce women's' hair care brand. She previously led the Bay Area office of Maveron Ventures.

Rob Kornblum:
Amy, maybe tell me a little bit about the founding of Madison Reed, specifically the co-founder group? Take me back to the beginning.

Amy Errett:
There were four of us...the other woman and I had worked in a previous company as the CEO and the CMO; I knew that we had that as a successful starting place. The other two people I knew from when I was a VC. I [had] opened and run Maveron's Bay Area office in between being a three-time entrepreneur, and Madison Reed.

So, one of those guys that I knew was an operator, an Entrepreneur-in-Residence that I brought into Maveron, and then the other guy had run one of our portfolio companies, and was thinking about what he was going to do next. So, we had preexisting trusting relationships. I'm the only one still here...it just became clear in the first year that one of the guys was going through a personal issue, so it just made sense for him to move on.

Then in year two, one of the other guys, it just became super clear that the business was scaling dramatically, and he was much more of a "When there's nothing, let me get there to be something." And, [he was] terrific at that, and didn't like the minutiae. So we kind of talked about him moving on, and he's founded another company. Then the other woman stayed here until just the beginning of this year, and again, felt like she wanted to go off and do something else after the business is just in a much bigger scaling mode.

As you the founding team, how did you find your first few hires who weren't founders [and] sell them on the opportunity? Given the number of companies in the Bay Area, how did you differentiate from lots of other start-ups?

We all had a pretty extensive existing network, so, a lot of it came from existing relationships...in the beginning this is really all about your network, which increases the probability that you will at least skip the first step, "Who are you and can I trust you?" We were able to use that network as a way to entice people.

How the heck were we going to convince engineers to come work at a place that was about women's hair color? So, [the] initial engineers were recruited out of General Assembly (*a company Amy had funded*) as people that needed their first engineering job.

We were venture-funded, so there was money in the bank, and I think that de-risks the scenario. It was a big idea. Some of us had done stuff before and had success. Then, we also got a very terrific CTO early, who came from Gap.com. He had built Rhapsody with someone who has now become our VP of engineering, and I convinced them to come as kind of a package. People thought I was nuts, like "That's too expensive, you don't need that in a company." But, the truth is I've always hired way ahead of the curve.

How did it work having four founders, which is a little larger than the norm? What was the investor feedback on that?

It was too many. I think we should have had a technical co-founder. We had some founders that were wonderful people but didn't add the kind of value that they should have added, and it was dilutive...I think we burned some cycles and some money by not getting that right in our first iteration, [raising capital before the technical hires]. Our first VP of engineering lasted four or five months, and then we found this CTO and VP of engineering, but we had to rebuild all the systems again...You can never go back and change anything, and the company is doing well, and life goes on, but if I was going to do it again, I wouldn't do that.

How did you know, or how did they know, either that the business was scaling past where they wanted to be or maybe their capabilities?

I'd been the CEO from the beginning and I was pretty open with them. So, these came out of fully transparent dialogues like, "Hey, it's not [just a feeling], here's some concrete examples of what's not [working]."

Like one of the folks was overseeing logistics and operations, and we had run out of things. [We had moved] one of the other co-founders from digital product, where that wasn't going well, to helping with recruiting, and that wasn't going well. So, every time we tried to take something else on, it was just obvious... that, [they were going through a personal issue], that their head wasn't in the game.

So, I would say that these conversations were really never like, "You must leave." They were really mutual in helping people get to a place where they could understand that maybe they just weren't liking it anymore. [Probably there will] be a day, if this is a public company or something like that, then I'm not the right person. That's okay. I just think it's a certain understanding, almost a certain maturity level and honesty, and a kind of radical authenticity, to have a conversation that demystifies it. Right? It's just honest feedback, like "Are you really happy?" And, how can people get in touch with their own egos and see what's best for the company and ultimately for them economically?

You have talked about transparency and other elements that sound important to you as a CEO. How early on did you focus on culture and values?

Day one. I think we were three weeks into the company as a group of people that called themselves, 'The Thomas Jefferson Group', and we holed ourselves up in one conference room, wrote the mission, and then the values and the subtenets of the values. They're the same mission and values the company has today, all over the wall.

Wow, that's great. Especially as you began to scale and bring in people (from outside the immediate people you knew), how did you reinforce those values?

So, the first thing is we have two in-house recruiters that have been here a while, and they really embody the culture. So, the first thing is, any [first] screen of a person has to start from the place of, are they a good cultural fit? Regardless of the content skills. Will this work for them and for us? Are those dialogues in the company something that they can understand? Does it resonate with them? Would that be a good fit for their motivation?

Then, the interviews are done with content in mind, [with] the direct boss or peers, but always reinforcing, "This is how we operate, here's what we do, here's what we don't do." Then, I meet every single person before we extend an offer...I know it's crazy, but I do.

I worked for a founder who did that up through 150 people.

Yeah, and so I believe, and I'm just screening for cultural fit.

What are the cultural elements that you're trying to screen for?

Team player is number one. Self-awareness, meaning they have an understanding that every interaction has something to do with yourself and the other person. A sense of purpose. We're a mission-driven company, our ingredients are low in chemical profile. Do they want to work somewhere where [caring and community service] is as important as anything else? Are they into being part of a community where people really care about each other, and invest in giving back?

I always ask the people one question... "Tell me something that happened in your life that didn't go well, and what did you learn from it?"

[One of our values] is love. Love for our customers, love for the community, love for each other...if somebody just says something like, "I don't understand what love has to do about work," then we know they're not a good fit.

It's interesting, there have been two schools of thought among the CEOs that I've spoken with. One who falls very squarely where you do that you've got to screen for [culture] on the way in, and others who say, "Actually, cultural fit is code for bias. I'm looking for culture-add, not necessarily culture-fit." What is your perspective on that?

Let's put it this way. When I'm trying to vet for our values the person has, I'm not vetting for style [or] are they going to think differently. I'm vetting for, are they here for the same reason that everyone else is here? How would they handle a really bad situation? Are they ethical people? Would they opt to make money over doing something that is not ethical?

So, it's super interesting, because it's really not that I'm vetting for [sameness], I'm vetting for a basic understanding. Like, the way I call it in my house, we have a set of family rules. It's like a guidepost for behaviors.

That makes sense. I appreciate the distinction. As you started to scale the business, how did you begin to put systems in place around hiring? In particular, as you get out of that product market fit phase, you get into a phase that I call the "Messy Middle."

One of the things that we did pretty quickly was hire a C-level team. That was super helpful, because we could block and tackle around organizational structure, and what level of responsibility the different jobs have, and who's making certain kinds of decisions. That was a big thing initially, which fell into hiring, [and] the responsibility for interviewing, the process for which we would find candidates. Just things like having an org chart, describing to people our benefits program, and how do we think about compensation?

We've done a ton of blocking and tackling. We are over 100 people, [but] the company is still suffering [from some growing pains], and we're in the midst of hiring our first senior HR person. I think one of the things that we're seeing is that we're still in the muck of doing it the old way.

So, we've had to hire some external recruiters. We've had a lot of support around our offer letters, and using Greenhouse (HR software), and some of the admin systems that can help you with candidate flow. We've had to put out performance appraisals...we're going to go to 500 people, and we're not prepared for it yet.

Yeah, different inflection point. How important was it for you as a second-time or third-time CEO to have been through that before, and know what you need to put in place a bit ahead of time?

Super important. I mean, I feel like part of the playbook is I actually have a pretty good sense or roadmap of how to see around the corner before we need to get there.

It all comes down to leadership, to people. It all comes down to preparing people for what's ahead, and getting their heads right before it happens...a lot of it is about forcing people to hire the right people before they think they need them, because if you build it, it will come. If you have a viable business, it all comes down to having people, right? I think one of the things in startups is that either you hire too fast, and you don't have the right people, or you don't hire fast enough, and then you're behind, you're over your skis.

Right, figuring that cadence out, or that timing out is challenging, especially the first time you go through it. How much time do you spend on hiring?

25% of my time.

Wow. So, a huge chunk. Specifically, are those on your direct reports, or are you still trying to build out the rest of the organization down below you?

It's on my directs, and then helping my directs, and pushing my directs [to look around that corner]. For some people that have never done it, it results in mistakes... they might not know what right looks like, and then you're hiring the wrong person, and then it comes back and bites you in the ass. But, I think the organization's getting better at that.

You guys are now at that stage where one of those things that breaks down is communication. How are you thinking about evolving that communication model and structure for continuing to communicate values and culture and strategy, develop the team as it grows?

I talk to the company every week.

We all have lunch together on Mondays, where I would really stand up every single Monday and talk to the entire company...I think that's been a huge advantage, because there is such a level of open authenticity and communication. There isn't ever a time where people [don't] hear our feelings. I would say that we overly communicate. So, we haven't seen that stuff breaking, however, we are opening retail [locations] all over the country, and I think that's where the challenges are going to be.

Right, and what are your thoughts around communicating with all those line employees, but also making sure they buy in on strategy and values and all the rest of that when they're super distributed?

If I had that answer for you ...That's the work that's being done right now.

I'm hiring a senior HR person who's done this before. We're starting to figure out how to do that in a way that includes people, but doesn't take them out of their daily routine. We're trying to figure out what are the most important things. We're trying to figure out how a store manager ends up knowing the Madison Reed way when they've never been here.

That's the really important stuff. And when you do your town halls or your Monday noon discussions, are they more updates or values and strategy?

They're half and half.

How do you keep that fresh? What are your tips for a CEO who's in that mode, like, you did this whole values and strategy bit for the company?

I'm always doing current things, so that keeps it fresh... I also take current situations as learning moments. That usually takes me down a path of talking about where we are developmentally. I am a huge believer of walking people through the stages of the company. I talk to them about why things are happening the way they are, to normalize them, so that people aren't feeling like, "What the hell is happening here?" versus, "Oh, this is right on track." [And] "here's what we need to watch for." I think that gives people a sense of reality and authenticity, and I think it makes them also feel safe.

So there are no surprises?

Right. After a week, there's a shit-load of things to talk about.

Is the expansion into retail and all the cultural pieces, is that your biggest organizational challenge right now?

Absolutely. Well, yes and in headquarters, we have a call center, which are hourly employees and [that's] growing. So, we have some very different constituencies within the company, and that is something that we spend a lot of time both talking about and thinking through culturally.

How do those constituencies interact?

They actually interact every day, it's fascinating. The call center is really positioned as the brand ambassador to the customer. So I think we've done a very good job of not making them [feel like] the bottom of the food chain. They all get stock. We pay them more than they would make externally...quite a few of those people have gotten significant promotions, and actually turned into salary employees and have their lives changed. So, we use that in a very authentic way as the aspiration for the company, and I think that really matters.

Yeah. Okay, so step above it for just a second. So, as a multi-time founder and venture capitalist, what's the number-one team mistake that you see founders make or that you think founders can avoid?

When you know about a person, you know. Anything that you do to [avoid making] the changes you need to make, as soon as you know you need to make them, is a disservice to the company. It's still enormously painful to me... But when you know, you know, and any rationalization just ends up being something that actually hurts the company, ultimately hurts the person, and certainly hurts coworkers.

Do you see that on the positive side, too?

You mean when you know that somebody deserves to be promoted? Yeah, totally. When you know that someone's terrific, you shouldn't wait to execute against that, but more times than not for founders, it's the other way.

It's a critical issue, because if you talk to most founders, I would bet you this is the thing in the rearview mirror that [they] realize they should have been doing.

Remote Teams

Companies are increasingly turning to remote employees, who work away from headquarters from their homes or co-working species, for mission critical work. This is happening more and more in Silicon Valley, New York, Boston and other startup hotbeds as the war for talent intensifies. Growing companies simply cannot find enough talent in their home location.

This can happen early on in a startup's life, but the need definitely grows as companies scale their hiring and the challenge of finding great people intensifies.

For instance, Rob Chesney of the Trunk Club, interviewed previously, offers perspective about the remote working experience:

> "We stayed centered in Chicago for a long, long time. Probably it wasn't until three years into my time with the company that we actually opened our first location...in Dallas, then D.C., then L.A., then New York, then Charleston. The only real people we had in those offices were sales people. Everyone else was central to Chicago."

According to research by talent marketplace Upwork, 63% of companies now have remote workers. More than half cited "access to talent" as the primary driving force behind the trend. Over 90% say hiring is more challenging in 2017 than it was previously.

One San Francisco venture capital firm, True Ventures, has even said that nearly every one of its companies has remote workers. "It has become a 'best-practice' for a

Silicon Valley startup,"[5] driven by the lower cost of living outside the Bay Area and the need for A+ talent.

The benefits of having remote employees include:

- The opportunity to get the best talent for a particular task, regardless of location
- The flexibility you offer employees enables you to attract high-end talent
- The possibility of lower costs, either through lower salaries or the reduction of recruiter fees

There are a number of key decisions that you need to make about remote employees. The first is whether you are seeking to be an entirely remote company, or if you will have a main headquarters location but also have remote employees.

If you do the latter, you have a headquarters location or a "base" that you can bring your remote employees. This can be a real benefit in forging relationships and face-to-face connection.

Hiring team members for remote teams needs to be done thoughtfully—not everyone will thrive in a remote setting, especially in a rapidly changing startup environment. Beyond their ability to do the work, make sure you screen for their ability to proactively build work relationships and trust remotely. Take time to check how the candidates have done in prior remote settings and do some reference checking with previous employers.

One way to assess prospects is by hiring them for project work before bringing them on full time. As suggested earlier, using small scale case studies in interviews is one

---

[5] San Jose Mercury News, 04/09/2018
https://www.mercurynews.com/2018/04/09/the-bay-area-broken-why-local-startups-are-hiring-outside-silicon-valley/

way to gauge the candidate's temperament. Actual work-for-hire projects will take this further and give you a good sense of your potential employee's skills and communication style.

Having remote team members increases the need for organization in your startup. Communication will be more difficult, so you need to account for this. You will need to make some adjustments including scheduling team meetings around audio and video conferencing equipment, keeping detailed work plans up to date, and checking in frequently.

When you decide to hire remote team members, you have to commit to tools and processes to support the entire team. The good news is that this is much easier to do today than even five years ago.

You will want a video conferencing solution like Zoom, a centralized document repository like Box or Dropbox, a team chat offering like Slack, and a lightweight project management tool like Asana or Trello. There are plenty of other choices for these types of tools, and lots more you can add.

Jay Friedman, COO of Goodway Group, has a 400-person distributed workforce.[6] Goodman suggests that you have to default toward documenting things:

> Think about how many impromptu in-person conversations you have in a week. In how many of those are agreements or decisions made? Usually quite a few, right? But these go undocumented, simply because both parties made eye contact and

---

[6] Fast Company, 06/22/2017
https://www.fastcompany.com/40432244/my-400-person-company-has-a-great-work-culture-and-we-all-work-remotely

talked about it in-person... Eye contact doesn't have enterprise value, though. Documentation does.

When joining our company, new employees are exposed to "the wiki." It has achieved a kind of ever-present, pervasive presence in our culture. Notes from every meeting are on the wiki. My one-on-ones with my direct reports are protected to just that person and me. But department notes, leadership team meeting notes, and most all other meeting agendas and notes are left open. This inspires trust and accountability, too. There are follow-up tasks on every page with the assignees called out.

These tools are great for communication and getting the work done. You will need to use some others, as well as devote time, to build and maintain culture among remote employees. Video conferencing and video training help communicate facial expressions. A "virtual workplace" like Sococo can increase the feeling of working side by side.

Lastly, don't underestimate the occasional plane trip to let people get face-to-face and build relationships in person. Friedman's company Goodway, does these in interesting places like Deer Valley, Utah.

"When people arrive, they're genuinely excited to see each other—hugs abound because we literally haven't seen each other in six months. For remote employees, seeing their work family can be as exciting as seeing extended families. And like any family reunion, come Friday, everyone is ready to head home."

Remote work arrangements do require effort for tools, and trips like these, but for most high-growth companies, these efforts are worth it to get access to the people they need, the "rocket fuel" for their startup.

Interview with Mark Godley, President, LeadGenius

Mark Godley is president of LeadGenius, an innovative B2B data company powered by human intelligence and machine learning. He was previously the President of HG Data.

Rob Kornblum:
We were talking earlier about whether you look to hire for culture or whether you think culture is more built by employees after they arrive. Secondly, we were talking about what defines a good culture and a couple of different examples so maybe you could tell me a little bit more about where you stand.

Mark Godley:
I believe culture is something that you don't do, it happens. Another way to say it is culture is an output, not an input. I think when I [try too hard to impact] culture, I end up doing what I would consider shallow experiences. If you do the trust falls event or bring in an outside speaker that people feel really good about, but 30 to 90 days later, there's no change. You bring in the bagels once a week. These are things that I would describe as really shallow, and not very impactful. That's when you're trying to [create] culture.

The way I try to do culture is much more long-term and deeper than that. To me, culture is finding a diverse group of people, understanding what their individual needs, motivations and goals are, and finding the overlap between all of those people, and in then that overlap becomes kind of where you build culture around.

I'm not just talking employees [as a stakeholder group]. I extend culture to stakeholder groups...Board of Directors, investors, customers, vendors, all of those entities. [They all] contribute to the culture that manifests itself internally in the organization and also the culture as it manifests itself in the external brand awareness in the greater marketplace.

How do you think about or distinguish the difference between company culture and values? Do you try to hire for values if you're not hiring for culture?

I think values are what you evaluate that creates the input and generates the output of culture. So I hire for characteristics, for traits, for values. I'm not hiring anesthesiologists [or brain surgeons]; I'm not hiring structural engineers where hard and fast skills like that take years and years of honing. I'm hiring for general business experts that have shown a degree of success and their skill set is flexible enough and it can be applied to my particular problem. By the way, one of the reasons I do this is I've made my last 10+ years and I'll make the next 10 years in the audacious startup embryonic startup environment. [Companies are] pre-revenue, A and B funding where I don't know what this company's going to look like six months to 18 months from now. I can't hire very narrowly for a job because I may find out that we've totally effed up and may need to do a pivot and if I've hired narrowly, that person may not end up coming with me.

That makes sense. We've talked about the best available athlete concept, for sure.

Now by the way, there are three things that I hire universally for across every rung of the org chart or any functional area and it goes back to [the idea that] these companies that are trying to do bold things against the odds, most of which are going to fail, and the three characteristics I look for are resilience, flexibility, and something I call "diffused leadership." Or put another way is quiet, silent, hidden leadership. It's leadership when no one else is looking...It's not getting up in front of the room and saying, "Charge" and "Follow me."

Interesting. How do you try to [interview and] hire for those three? [How] do you screen for those, because they are important from a value perspective?

I try to create a very experiential interview process that tests for it. To me, I will literally create scenarios that try to see how people will react in these situations... say, "I can't talk right now. We have to reschedule." I'll bring someone in expecting to meet with someone, have them have to change gears and meet with an entirely different functional unit. I'm trying to create in the hiring process a little microcosm of what their world will be like, a fast-moving startup where priorities are going to get changed and you need to be able to change with it. I don't know if that makes any sense.

Yes, certainly for the flexibility part. How about for resilience?

Resilience? I'll tell someone they screwed up to see how they'll react. I'll literally lie to them, and say, "You know what, your interview with [person x] did not go very well. Let me tell you why." Are they going to ask questions that get into what happened and change their view, are they being reflective, are they going to end up in the fetal position crying, are they going to look at themselves and say, "Can I talk to that person again because I think if I had a second chance, I would address that differently." I purposely create adversity in the interview process to see how they react to it.

Let me give you a real example from this week. We had a guy come up that everybody loved face-to-face and the last step of the process was the gauntlet, something I've become known for. I say, "Rob, I need two hours of your time and you need to be at a computer. In the first hour you'll be on your own. You've got 60 minutes to prepare for a meeting [with me] and the meeting is what you understand LeadGenius to be, how you understand the role you're interviewing for, and why do you think you're qualified." You would be shocked at what happens at the other end of that hour. By the way, I only do this for people that I am literally ready to hire.

About 50% of the people don't get an offer. My team this week said, "Mark, I would have hired this guy after last week's interview sight unseen but he absolutely struck out horribly." He would not survive here because those kinds of pressure-filled situations happen every day, and he crumbled.

We talked a little bit earlier about this panel that you were on. I want to understand your thoughts around this panel in terms of employee needs, which I find fascinating.

I've been at LeadGenius for a year. This is the first time in 10 years that I am managing and guiding a lot of millennials. I'm 49 years old. I am literally the oldest employee at our 48-employee company. So about this panel, Rob, and it's me and two other people speaking and they're just going on and on about how culture is about meeting employee expectations—what they were really talking about was making people happy, that everyone should love coming to work...a lot that I hear from this panel was echoing what I'm hearing from these millennials.

For me, culture is not about everybody loving coming to work. At the panel, I posed the same question, which is this: I've been hired by investors and board members to make a company successful and a successful company doesn't necessarily mean a culture where everybody loves coming to work every day.

The examples I brought up at this panel are two companies that I admire tremendously, Amazon and Netflix...I'm a stockholder because I've been such a satisfied consumer. If I could one day run a company that was compared to them externally, my business life would have been much more wildly successful than I ever imagined, but both of those companies have been vilified because of their culture. I'm sure you've read the hit piece on Amazon—that the *New York Times* did and Netflix had the famous HR manifesto about culture which people externally have just said it's an example of nothing good. I brought up this point about culture being about company success, and if you focus too much on this happiness piece, I think you end up in this very shallow area of bagels every week—

And posters on the wall?

—and posters on the wall, when to me, culture is about who are the stakeholder groups, what are they trying to achieve, and where is the overlap; if there's not overlap, that's major red flag to me and certainly in startup. When I'm brought into startups, I typically find that there's an overlap and I spend my first year creating consensus. What are we trying to achieve: customers, employees, vendors, investors, shareholders, community? [Without] everyone on that same page, I don't think I can build long-term culture that will have the resilience and flexibility to be successful.

That makes sense. One of the things about both of those companies is their strong tendency to challenge people coming from a place of trust, that people are capable and can do what's asked of them but you've got to ask a lot...At least that's my understanding. Are those things that you try to emphasize?

Completely, completely, and when I'm talking to employees, I'm asking not about their job title but I'm asking them, "Where do you want to be in 10 or 20 years?" If they haven't thought about that, that's a red flag to me but I ask them to think about this and then if they can't articulate that, I ask about how can what you're achieving what we want you to achieve in your current role that you may have for another six months [or] four years. How can we design something that could be a small incremental step towards that long-term career/life/personal goal or vision you've outlined? That's what I'll try to tap into. It's not "did you like coming in today." I think, to your point, if people can be challenged and feel like they're growing and getting better, that is going to have a degree of ... long-term commitment that I need from an intimate group of people trying to defy the odds.

That makes sense. I want to shift gears and talk about executive hiring and executive team-building. How do you go about trying to hire non-founding executives into reasonably early-stage companies, especially where they've got such varied experiences that you make sure their values align?

A couple things here. First, because I'm working in small companies, 100 employees plus or minus, these exec teams are pretty small. It's four to 10 people. I'm not having to hire dozens or hundreds of senior executives. As a result, I am often tapping into my personal network like the relationship you and I have built, though I think the first time we spoke you were calling someone for a job reference—

Yeah, that's right.

—and within 10 minutes, I was like, "Wow, like I like this guy" and you and I both went out of our way to build a personal relationship. So, I kind of collect people; when I need to make an executive hire, I draw upon that network at my first step and I probably get 80% of the people there. Now both you and I are white males, middle-aged. I think the problem with tapping into your network is you could end up with an

I try to build my network in a very diverse, robust fashion and I've had a diverse career, from the outdoor industry to the nonprofit sector and now I work in Silicon Valley. I actually ran a nonprofit that worked in poor inner-city communities with people of color, so... It wasn't all Silicon Valley. Back to the point earlier, I look for characteristics rather than prior experience.

That makes sense. What do you emphasize in areas where your network just isn't producing, do you turn to a search firm or your board? When you get that team together, who haven't worked together with each other, how do you try to build teamwork and trust among them?

To the point of interviewing, getting to know someone...When I look at their lengthy profile, I don't look at their experience. I look at what they posted and liked, what articles they wrote, what groups they're a part of, what other people said about them, where they worked, their title, what they've accomplished in their role. Getting back to characteristics, hiring not for skill set or experience but for aptitude. When I interview, most people have their ready-made "let me tell you what I did the last three years." I say, "No." I ask, "What do you want to know about us?" I want to know have they done their homework, what questions are they asking, and by the way, when they're interviewing me and the company I work for, I'm interviewing them.

What are they asking about, are they listening actively, do the digressions we do make sense and what am I learning from? My interview processes seem very unstructured, let alone what I said earlier about throwing monkey wrenches in the mix. It's very experiential but I'm trying to get below the surface of your last employer and title. Let's get deeper than that. As far as when they come on board, let me flip the table on you a little bit and answer it this way. When I was hired at HG Data, I was the first senior-level non-founder hire...for a group of people that had worked together for eight years at a prior entity. That was intimidating as hell. How do I come into this [mostly male] band of brothers? How do I build my personal credibility? I had to go into this organization and build personal credibility, respect. and a bank of relationships that I could draw upon when I had to tell them their baby was ugly.

At LeadGenius, I was brought on board by the VCs, not by the exec team; I was very cognizant of the fact that I couldn't come in and start dictating. I had to build relationships with that senior team so that even though the board dictated it, I had to earn it from underneath me before I could start making serious decisions.

Okay. What are the things that you do now as a leader to try to promote or develop trust and cohesiveness among your direct reports and your management team? How are they working?

Yes, I do things formally, whether it be meetings or offsite or all the usual suspects, but I encourage the much more powerful informal stuff. It's people going out to dinner, it's people going for a run together before a conference. When people come to me, given that I'm the CEO, you know things end up at my desk. When someone comes to me with a frustration or a complaint to resolve, the way I typically resolve it is forcing them to safely have the direct dialogue without me in the middle.

What I'm trying to do, Rob, is build this interlocking web of relationships, not a hub-spoke-type design, that does not have either me or the formal org chart as the hub. Like I just described the situation with the CEO as the hub; I don't want the senior team as the hub. That's this concept of diffused leadership. By the way, given that we have 500 people around the globe in 38 countries, this concept of diffusion is having your culture manifest itself in quiet interactions that will never bubble up to anyone's visibility. That's when your culture is a living, breathing thing. It's an output, not an input.

Right, right. Maybe all the more important for LeadGenius than other prior companies, just because of the dispersion of your talent.

Right. Now, I think I've become very sensitive to this because... I have only worked or lived at headquarters location for four of the 30 years I've spent in the working career.

I have always been remote, even when I've been on the senior team. To survive, I've had to develop a unique ability to be effective and proficient, either managing remotely or being managed remotely. When people talk about remote, they talk about WebEx and Slack...There's a concept of [being] remote but physically present. I think more and more there's this concept of asynchronous interaction, not in real time. Most people are familiar with destroying culture asynchronously. It's when you send that email in the heat of the moment thoughtlessly or just because you're multitasking that ends up destroying a situation. We've all done that.

Sure.

I'm thinking the opposite. How do you lead, how do you build culture in an asynchronous fashion? Because more and more, that's what our world is. It's not 9 to 5 Monday through Friday.

I'm taking Friday afternoon off because I want to see my kids graduate from high school and you know I'm going to make it up over the weekend.

How do you think about that asynchronous communication? Are there things that you do both as the CEO and in coaching your direct reports and their directs, to build that cultural element and that asynchronous trust?

I'm not saying we're going to go asynchronous 24/7 but I think if you build up enough individual relationships and organizational connectivity, that web, it will allow you to do things asynchronously that don't have the risk of other environments. I'll give you two examples. I promoted a guy, not via Slack but through instant message, on Sunday morning. Three years ago, I would have thought I have to wait until 10 a.m. on Monday for maximum impact so I want to do it when everyone's around.

I've built up enough of this concept of diffusion, and because of the design of the organization I came into...in bed Sunday morning at 6:30 a.m., literally from my phone pasting the final edit of the announcement into a company chat and posting it. It sounds like a small example but... Again, go back five or 10 years, an employee might say, "Wow, I'm not going to get the full impact of the glory of my promotion," but that was not a thought here.

By the way, we pass out bad news in an asynchronous fashion, letting someone go, firing someone, [or] pivoting the business. We might have a recorded meeting where we don't have a quorum, someone else can listen to it on their time. Knowing that, the next time I see someone who missed the meeting, he might come up to me and say, "Mark, I want to talk to you about that call I listened to. You said something that bothered me." Again, that web is strong enough that we can shift riskier events or communications to other forums, knowing that that web is going to bring us back together to rebuild if it did have a negative effect, Does that make any sense or am I talking too much in metaphors?

It does make sense and we've kind of segued to this remote team idea. I'd like to understand a little bit more about how you go about building that web or ensuring the strength of it, as opposed to things you do once you know that it does exist? How you manage once the web is there is different than how you make sure it is there.

It goes back to the bigger picture. You can do these things once the culture has become defined and understood by everyone. Again, not that everyone's happy but all stakeholders understand what we're trying to accomplish. I have built personal relationships with enough people to understand how it parallels the organizational goals.

I have challenged them to do some of that diffused leadership, and I expect them with their direct reports, based on what Mark has modeled for me in our one-on-one interactions... to be thinking about what we're trying to accomplish as a company. How do I need to conduct myself? That [has] a ripple effect, so probably a third of my schedule is one-on-one's, both formal and informal. Another third of my schedule is market-basing activities, and the last third of my schedule is formal meetings, more group.

Do you think your team leads, whether their VPs or directors, spend that much time doing the same for their teams, does it translate down? And is that more so because it's remote or just because that's the way that you guys manage?

I think both are a necessity because we're so geographically dispersed, but even in our Berkeley office, it's a concept of remote. I mean I try to encourage a working environment that doesn't expect you to build your life around work but expects you to build work into your life. The difference there is we've got 40 people that work in this office. The other 25 are working but they're not physically here.

You look at what's happened to Yahoo in the last year and IBM about this concept of getting rid of remote. To me that's lunacy, an example of companies in crisis who had a culture problem. If you don't trust your people to be doing what you'd expect them to be doing when you're physically present, you've already lost.

Often, when I hear about an employee doing something [positive] that they didn't expect would ever come out, I will publicly recognize that quiet leadership, not just hitting the number, as a way to reinforce for everyone that that's what we expect.

That's cool. How do you recreate with your diffuse team the magic of the face-to-face, whether you're looking somebody in the eyes, brainstorming at the whiteboard, or even just the overall let's grab lunch together or break bread?

We use the typical tools that have become commonplace at least in Silicon Valley, but with a slight difference. In five minutes, I'm walking into a recurring meeting that will have people from Berkeley, Pittsburgh, Denver, the Ukraine, and from the Philippines, okay? We're going to do a conference call but it's culturally required that your video is on. We don't care if you're in your boxers the first time, or if you have dirty laundry on the back of the chair behind you. We don't give a shit. But it's important that we bring that physicality and a little bit of the non-verbals, not as much as if you're in the room.

Another quick example that I just instituted. We had two different organizational chat platforms. I said that's ridiculous, we'll put everyone from different organizations on the same platform. We just moved a month ago to RocketChat, an open source version.

So you don't see that there's a magic, I guess, to that in-person element?

I don't. Rob, again, keep in mind that only four of 30 years have I been 40 hours face-to-face. I have had multiyear relationships with people whom I have never met to this day. I trust them and value them and include them as much as someone who I've been attached to the hip, so I think I've just been hyper-challenged in this area and geography means nothing to me.

So you know what can work and you make it work.

Now again, you have to work extra hard with more of the face time, the screen share stuff, because the impromptu bumping into someone at the coffee pot is less.

It just doesn't happen by chance but if you work at it, you can build that, you can build a relationship that's just as meaningful as face-to-face.

Everything Breaks at 100

I had not originally planned to include this chapter, but multiple conversations with founders prompted me to do so. (Hat tip to Rob Biederman, Founder and co-CEO of Catalant Technologies, who first suggested the idea. His book, Reimagining Work, is a great read for founders and all executives.)

No matter how well your company is working, all rapidly growing startups reach a point where the size and complexity begin to overwhelm the team and processes that you have in place. For some reason, that appears to be around 100 employees. Many founders such as Sean Byrnes (interviewed previously) have commented on this phenomenon and the early warning signs.

> "Well, firstly, I think if communication breaks at 100, [honestly] it actually broke earlier than that, you just didn't notice. I think it just forces you to deal with it, because the wheels have already started coming off, the truck hasn't gone over the side of the road yet...I think that as a company grows, [of] the biggest two risks that I've ever seen, one is a failure to set expectations about these kind of inflection points, because companies shift.

> When you go from 10, to 20, to 50, to 100, to 200, to 500, things change. You go from knowing everybody in the office, to maybe having met everybody in the office once, to not having any idea who the hell these people are. And if you don't get *very* proactive and set the expectations with people that this change is happening [and how], they can react very badly to it. Even if you hire the kind of people I'm describing that are very adaptable, nobody likes surprises.

The second thing that's really critical, as you're growing, is you can no longer rely on informal things that may have worked. It may have been easy to convey the vision of the company to everybody when you're 10 people, because you see them every week. When you have 150 people, you can no longer rely on that kind of informal communication channel that got you started. You have to get much more structured, because if you aren't structured, the information won't disseminate."

So what breaks and what can you do about it?

- Communication between leaders and the company
- Communication between departments like sales & marketing or product management and engineering
- Culture changes or gets diffused
- Processes break down
- Multiple offices
- International expansion
- Remote workers change communication norms

Oxford University anthropology professor Robin Dunbar contends that humans can only maintain relationships with 150 people or fewer. The so-called "Dunbar's number" is based on his observation of the number of villagers in hunter-gatherer societies, the average village size in England, and the average parish size of Hutterite and Amish settlers in America. There are many other examples, the most notable being in the military, where the "company" size tends to be 120-180 soldiers.

Regardless of the number, whether it is 100 or 150, CEOs and management teams need to contend with the issues of communication and management as they scale the business. Many of these issues could begin to kick in at 50 or 75 employees as well.

Kevin Delaney, founder of startup media company Quartz[7], says:

> "In retrospect, it's easy to see why our flat management structure, with limited hierarchical levels and consensus-based decision-making, ceased being as effective as it once was. Too often, our staff was stalled because it wasn't clear who was responsible for moving a decision forward. Employees craved more feedback and career development than managers in the flat structure had bandwidth to provide.
>
> Also, information about and ownership of our strategy, norms, and values weren't spread adequately across our staff, as our ad hoc approach to internal communications showed its limitations."

Patty McCord, the Chief Talent Officer at Netflix during their early days, calls it the "stand on a chair" number. When the CEO in the company meeting needs to stand on a chair to address the troops, and someone in the back says, "We can't hear you," then you are probably having difficulty communicating and need to rethink your methods.

The CEO *and* the executive leadership team need to have regular communication to articulate where the company is going and also find ways of being open to feedback.

Software company Hubspot faced these issues as the company scaled. CEO Brian Halligan, faced significant challenges with internal communication and head negative

---

[7] Published interview- https://qz.com/846530/something-weird-happens-to-companies-when-they-hit-150-people/

feedback from employees[8]. The internal Net Promoter Score (NPS) of the company as rated by the employees had dropped from 55 to 29 in one year as the company had grown from under 100 employees to over 150 employees.

Most of the issues and complaints that employees surfaced were around communication. The employee comments included:

- Our internal communications need a big overhaul given our massive growth.

- We're a mid-sized company acting like a startup so the level of change can be whiplash-inducing. It's hard to know what you're supposed to be doing day to day and harder to know what's coming down the pipe.

Halligan dug in over the next year to address the communication issues. He focused on:

- Over-communicating
- Being a good presenter
- Being a good writer
- Being "around"
- Being conscious of body language
- Delegating and empowering

So what does it mean to "over-communicate"? My opinion, echoed by many of the successful founders I have interviewed, is that the CEO needs to frequently repeat the mission, strategy and values of the company to employees.

---

[8] Medium post, Brian Halligan -
https://thinkgrowth.org/something-broke-when-we-passed-the-100-employee-mark-bfa922424e6d

The challenge with this is that the employees may tune out the same message delivered repeatedly in the same way. One way to overcome this is for CEOs to develop a communication plan that varies the audience, the method of communication (emails, written memos, speeches, PowerPoints, etc.) and the presenter. It might be the CEO in a town hall meeting, followed by the CTO in an email, then a different founder via an internal blog post. Repetition of the mission, values and strategy is important.

Multiple Offices

As startups grow, it is common for them to open one or more remote offices. Common reasons for a second or third office could be that the company does a small acquisition, or needs to access another talent pool, or gets closer to customers (such as International expansion).

It is true that multiple offices exacerbate the issues of communication, culture, and process that happen around 100 employees. Imagine how tough it is to manage communications across time zones or countries. The challenges of multiple offices are very similar to those of remote employees.

One phenomenon that can happen in multiple offices is the development of office "cliques." Distinct office cultures or personalities can be okay, but sometimes will result in an "us versus them" mentality that should be eliminated.

So what can a founder do?

- Make sure the remote office hiring has input from the home base.

- Send new remote employees to HQ for training and onboarding. It is so much easier to pick up the phone and hash out an issue when people already know each other through face-to-face interaction.

- Schedule time for the CEO and other senior management team to be present in the remote office, doing executive offsites, recognizing remote employees for their contributions in person, and simply dropping in on occasion.

Process Breakdown

In addition to communication challenges, it is quite common for internal operations of the company to become much more cumbersome as the business scales but internal processes do not keep up.

Every process—including sales, HR and onboarding, finance and expense management, product management, and customer interactions—strains the business as it grows from a small handful of people to a large entity. This is totally normal. Rethinking these processes with a 12 to 18-month time horizon should match the expansion of the business and current size and structure.

Interview with Rob Biederman, Founder & Co-CEO, Catalant

Rob Biederman is founder and co-CEO of Catalant Technologies, a human capital marketplace which provides on-demand skills and expertise for corporations worldwide.

Rob Kornblum:
Tell me a bit about the founding of Catalant.

Rob Biederman:
Sure, so it was obviously a slightly atypical founding story because we started as a class project at Harvard Business School. The project was quite explicitly to start a revenue-producing business in a really quick way, so I think we had all told about eight weeks to go from idea generation to revenue. It felt a little absurd, but I also think that a lot of that was responsible for why we were able to get the idea off the ground so quickly when a lot of people had tried fairly similar ideas without any real traction. It wasn't the Harvard Business School of best practices guide for building a better team with different skill sets, everybody's experience was basically the same or not useful at all: consulting, banking, private equity. I know we had a guy who been an oil field engineer which wasn't that relevant for what we were doing.

But I also think in a weird way, having nobody who really had any marketable skills made us pretty scrappy and hungry, instead of "thoughtful" or "strategic"... there was a lot of dirty traction for the first while, which was really a big benefit for us.

Right, and were all the four founders who were part of startup company the same people who'd been part of the class project? Or did you swap out folks that you thought you might need?

When we have any group of people, there's going to be varying levels of passion. We swapped in one and out three... we were doing a spring break at the fourth guy's ski house in Colorado. And Pat and I were so compelled by the business that we basically refused to go out with everybody to dinner, and so we stayed back and worked on the project. And basically, he was immediately [thinking], "Whatever they're working on that's so important, maybe I want to get involved with that."

Right, a lot of times when teams come together, you sort of break apart quite often, so there's incompatibility as the stresses build. Do you guys think about that in terms of knowing, besides the HBS connection, that you'd work well together?

In a weird way, the fact that we were all friends beforehand was actually a really positive thing for us. To a large extent, we are really able to cut through a lot of the crap; the trust and camaraderie is one reason why we worked so hard on the project at first. It felt like a more productive version of the hanging out we typically did. Five years later, still working with one of my closest friends. I've never had a day where I've thought, "I can't believe I have to go into work today. Some of that is pure passion for the idea, but honestly a lot of it is getting the chance to work with somebody that I like and respect so much.

Got it. I think obviously you have an unusual situation with co-CEO's, which is different than other co-founder [situations].

Yeah, I think you're not going to have too many peer relationships in your life where one person truly has no positional authority over the other, I suppose outside of marriage. There can be frustrating moments... [Being co-CEOs] with Pat, it really forces me to be at the top of my game; he can't overpower me, I can't overpower him. And so if I'm wrong about something, I don't win the argument, or if I am right but I articulate my feelings poorly, I also lose the argument.

How much of that dialogue happens in public, as part of the management team, and how much happens behind closed doors?

I'd say probably 80 to 90% is behind closed doors. I wouldn't say we're religious about making sure that they don't see any conflict between us, but it's never interpersonal conflict. I don't see any risk to airing substantive disagreements with one another as long as they're fact-based or merit-based, not personal. I think most of time, though, when it's something that's really related deeply to the strategy of the company, we try to hash it out a privately beforehand.

Right, makes sense. As you guys hired your first five to 10 people who were not founders, how did you sell them on the opportunity? How did you differentiate from the other hundreds of startups that people can join?

Obviously, every founder believes that their company is special. For our first really important hires, the case we always made, if we were successful, we might really actually provoke a pretty meaningful change and help people live their lives. And this was the kind of company that could really become a movement versus a lot of undoubtedly very successful companies but ones who have a pretty narrow selling market and piece of technology and value prop instead of much more of an idea. And then I think for getting a group of people at the right phase in their career, looking for the right opportunity to lead. That was compelling.

I'd say it's probably the case that most people who found companies and attract VC backing fall into probably one or the other box of just a technologist, or a really amazing smart computer or sales person. And in the case of our company, we really had neither. Since weren't good at anything other than raising money, we were willing to give a relatively high degree of autonomy to basically every functional expert we hired. And I think people at the stage of their career where they're really ready to take on a leadership role found that to be very compelling.

Shifting gears a little bit toward scaling; you first gave me the idea for everything breaks at 100, some have said 150. So tell me more specifically about that, what breaks? Where have you focused in terms of needing to put in place either process, communication, or culture?

So up to 75 people, particularly when you have multiple co-founders, it's actually relatively easy to keep everybody on the same page and aligned. The chance is high that most people are having a conversation with a co-founder [on most days]. I think what we found was you don't need to be super formal or super deliberate about organization or strategy when lots of really good, unplanned interactions happen anyway.

Obviously the numbers here are a little abstract... it is really hard to know when it actually has broken ... the chance that those meaningful interactions are happening all the time, that they're [hearing] the right things, goes down after 100.

We had a speaker in last week who [described] the CEOs [as] sitting right in the center of a circle. Imagine the company as a really big wheel, and the founders and CEOs are in the center. And everybody else is at the edges. Relatively small changes to us can have a huge, pronounced impact at the edges of the circle and can really throw you for a loop.

And I think that's where you start to get some of these feelings, like "why am I not on the same page" or "it's not important to the founders of this company that I know what's going on." And getting everybody in the company up to speed about some fact is often not the most efficient thing to do, whether for expediency's sake or confidentiality.

So, as you've managed that transition through 50 to 100, and where you are now, what have you done specifically differently to manage communication at that scale?

Well, we've gotten a lot more proactive and deliberate about... reviewing everything with the whole company [at certain key moments]. So, we do it offsite twice a year, in August and February. That's really in line with the launch of the new half fiscal year. And then every quarter after the board meeting, we just take the whole company through the board deck.

First of all, I think that kind of transparency is fairly uncommon, but we also want people to understand what we're telling the board. The promise we always make, if it happens in a board meeting and it's not about personnel or compensation, is "You're going to know about it." And I think that helps bring people into the tent, partially because the [attraction] of being in a company like ours is that you might be interested in being a founder or a VC or joining some other company and sharing some of the lessons you've learned at ours.

Do you guys think about yourselves that way, as being a launching point for other entrepreneurs? Do you sell that as part of your hiring process?

Definitely. I think one of our old corporate cultural principles was "Enable entrepreneurship." That really took the form of enabling our customers to be more innovative and nimble, allowing our experts or supply side to draw up exactly the kind of career they wanted. Most importantly, with our full-time employees, it facilitated them to be both entrepreneurial internally in how they work and function but then also to be potentially, literally, joiners of early stage companies in the future. I think that's inextricable from the value prop of a company like this, at a phase like ours. I think you have to be selling something a little bigger than just salary and some amount of equity. But also, employees will be effectively going to startup boot camp for however many years that they're with us.

So what have you done to maintain and reinforce some of the other cultural elements beyond entrepreneurial, specifically as you've scaled?

We've actually zeroed in on three specific ones that operate the three levels of your interactions with the company. We think that the first and most important level is almost like a very personal code, within yourself; our principle is be excellent. So not only try to win the game every day, but try to play the game expertly and do whatever you can to get better and aggressively pursue your own self-improvement. The second is how you operate within a small group of people in the company. At the team level, the principle is to be a force multiplier, so do whatever you can to make your peers better and be somebody that makes other people great. And the last is how the entire company operates as whole.

What we wanted was a set of corporate principles and cultural values; if everybody played a perfect game on those three principles, it would massively increase the chances of success or really decrease the chance of failure. And if you think about what it looks for a company that's doing all three of those things really well, when people are excellent, people are making each other better, and they're all collectively throwing the ball to the end zone, I can't help but imagine that companies that have done that really well have typically worked pretty well.

Do you ever feel like it's a trade-off, the balance between those cultural elements and the skill elements or traits that you need?

Of course. I think the most difficult trade-off that we've had to face many times, the gut-wrenching decisions, are the great individuals who don't want to be part of a team. It's almost always the case that we can do better [in the short term] with an excellent person, even if they're not so collaborative or they're not so helpful for their peers. But in general, there's a pretty big cost to having folks like that around.

I [call it] the person who breaks a lot of glass. Somebody has to walk around behind them and sweep up the glass. But if they're excellent and you let them stick around or worse yet give them a bonus, people see that and model that behavior...

Yeah. It's funny, the implicit power of suggestion in corporate cultures is, for better or worse, like raising children mimicking their parents. It works well in the upstart when people are modeling good behaviors; other people see that an unfair share of the benefits accrue to those people. And they usually try to replicate those behaviors. When, for lack of a better word, assholes are allowed to run wild, people realize that that's tolerated. For a lot of people, it's just a lot simpler to be a jerk. So we have to deal with the consequences of that.

As well as how people achieved their own goals and their team's goals, do you measure and try to value fit elements in the review process, or only on the entry?

So we're actually in the process of moving the entire review system to align with those three values, probably something like 40/40/20. Like in sales, the definition of excellence is pretty clear: you hit your goal. The first is really *how well* did you execute, relative to the resources that you had and the reasonableness of your mission, and the second and third will catch... I think the audacity is probably the one that's a little hardest to measure; we probably will be able to recognize it really well on the high side, and escalate the people just killing it to their peers. On the low side, it might stick out, with most people falling somewhere in between. So I think that's a good way to create more positive behavior.

Sure, sure. I think the best practice that I've seen and been part of is what do you do along some of those dimensions. The person who's crushing their goals, but not crushing the fit piece or the cultural elements and then the reverse of that. What are your remediation plans for either or both?

Yeah, for the extreme high performers (on putting on the personal and multipliers side) was we had the first time ever Founders Awards at the most recent offsite. Pat and I, in a completely undemocratic process, really looked into people who really deserved to be elevated and held as an example above their peers, particularly on the force multiplication. When we announced it in kind of a dramatic way, I think everybody realized that it was definitely true that those people deserved recognition for doing much more than their fair share of benefit in that area.

That's excellent. So, as we talk about scaling, I'm curious how much time you and Pat allocate to hiring. Maybe on a weekly basis, what are the things you're doing in terms of actual hiring-related tasks?

So even though it sounds inefficient, one thing that we actually spend a lot of time doing is the cold outbound to priority candidates for priority roles.

I think we've just seen that two of us recruiting on LinkedIn, with coffee chats, have a much better ability to get tentative engagement than our recruiting team, even with the exact same messages and phone calls. Not to diminish their role, but I think it just reflects that people want to feel special in being recruited by founders of the company.

Absolutely, yeah. So, beyond the executive roles that are reporting to you, how much time are you guys spending to build out of the rest of the team? What are your tasks related to that?

A lot of time is used by directly mentoring team members with how they interact with others. So we don't defer a lot of that; we are the primary mentor in a skip level way for a lot of the really high-performer potentials on the team. You can really only get out of that what you put into it.

I believe you've opened multiple offices now. How do you think about communication and culture between other offices, remote employees, and remote contractors in terms of reinforcing the cultural elements there?

Yeah, that's been really hard, and I think we haven't done a great job of that. We've tried quite a few times with remote offices, and none of them have really worked out well. Partly, it's just hard to keep everybody on the same page, especially when you aren't yet ready to make the massive tech investment to get a good outcome. It's a work in progress. I'm not sure I have anything positive to say about our experiences. Right now, we don't have remote offices at this point outside of Boston, though we have a few employees who sometimes work from elsewhere.

Okay. What are the tech pieces that you think would assist?

Pretty much around remote conferencing and whatnot.

Got it, and what's the total employee headcount?

About 145.

I think investing a lot in tech is undoubtedly something we'll have to do. It's just so hard to pull off that I'm nervous for the day that we really have to do that and can't get around it. I think it's really hard to do well, and/or just really expensive.

So, any last pieces of advice for founders, in terms of building out your team, building out culture, making sure you don't hit that 50 to 100-person road bump?

Yeah, I think communicating that passion about what you're doing throughout the process, not being afraid to potentially skew slightly less professional. That [may] sound kind of vomit-worthy founderish...I think a lot of the reason that we've been able to [hire] people, that you wouldn't have expected us to be able to [hire], has been that people have gotten swept up in how wildly passionate we are about this space. And startups are not something to be blasé about. If you're going to be blasé about your job, you can work at a law firm or investment banking. I generally think that people who are going to get good outcomes in startup situations are ones who are not afraid to wear their excitement on their sleeves...especially when you're operating in a space that doesn't exist. Nothing here's going to be easy for a really long time.

Putting It into Action

Get Clear on Your Values

Discuss, agree on, write down, and communicate your values to your entire company. Use them as a primary screening mechanism in hiring, and also consider using them as part of your review process. Much more than "culture fit," alignment of values is critical in startup hiring.

Put Together a One-Pager on Your Hiring Brand

Focus on the key questions:

- What does our company represent to prospective employees who don't know us?

- Why do they want to work here?

Make sure that makes it to your web site in text, or preferably in video; plan how to communicate it in your interview process.

Build a Hiring Process

A hiring process only needs to be as complex as your business. Start small and simple; use a wiki or a Google Doc. Define what you are looking for and the "success outcomes." Focus on consistency, communication, and speed.

Improve Your Interviewing

Regular question-and-answer interviewing is a very poor predictor of job performance and tends to focus on likeability. Because we tend to like people similar to us, it also reinforces group think and de-emphasizes diversity.

Behavioral interviewing, on the other hand, reveals more about how candidates have acted in situations. Job simulations, or "experiential interviewing," can be the best indicator of both skills and temperament.

Build a Pipeline

Get into a habit of speaking with "A players" in your network, and in your second-degree network (your network's network). Keep notes. Follow up. Have good conversations and spread the word about the good things happening at your company.

Make Decisions About Recruiters

Some CEOs use recruiters more, some less, some not at all. This is a matter of cost, funding, and personal preference. If you decide to do without, or bring recruiting in house, help your company get *really good* at recruiting.

Onboard Well

Help employees come up to speed quickly, learn your company and its people, learn your values and strategy, and facilitate their transition through effective onboarding. It will pay off in the long run, and reduce the chance of someone bouncing quickly due to a bad experience

For More Information

Please consider leaving a review on Amazon. I would be so appreciative:
https://www.amazon.com/dp/B07DHYMCRF

To access the bonuses associated with this book:

The bonuses are 100% free for readers of this book.

You get access at
www.entrepreneurrocketfuel.com/bonus

This is what you will receive:

Culture & Values worksheet

Top hiring and culture tips from Founders & CEOs

Personal Operating Manual for new employees

Hiring Pipeline Worksheet for CEOs and Founders

Examples of good "Careers" pages

Examples of Good Job Descriptions

And more

You can get everything at
www.entrepreneurrocketfuel.com/bonus

To work with Rob Kornblum as a coach:
http://www.startlaunchgrow.com/workwithme

To hire Rob Kornblum as a speaker for your event:
http://www.startlaunchgrow.com/speaking

Follow Rob on social media:
Twitter: https://twitter.com/rkorny
Instagram: https://www.instagram.com/startlaunchgrow/
Facebook:
https://www.facebook.com/groups/467704746989314/

Acknowledgements

I would like to thank my family, and especially my wife Suzie, and a number of colleagues who helped encourage me, helped organize my thoughts, and offered emotional and other support.

The following people graciously granted me time for interviews, sharing their stories and thoughts about startup teams, as well as opening their networks and making introductions.

Rob Biederman

Sean Byrnes

Rob Chesney

Lew Cirne *

Neil Costa

Jeff Crowe

Amy Errett

Mark Godley

Steve Hafner

Edith Harbaugh

David Mandell *

Art Papas *

Jothy Rosenberg

Lisa Skeete Tatum

prior interviews adapted for this book

I am deeply grateful for their time and for everyone who supports the startup community.

Made in the USA
Monee, IL
13 July 2023